T0006429

THE LITTLE BOOK OF JOY

MAGIC CAT PUBLISHING

NEW YORK

JANUARY 1
NEW YEAR'S DAY

Today is the first day of a brand-new year.
It's full of possibilities.

Take out a box of colored pencils and a fresh piece
of paper. You might know exactly what you want to
draw. Or you might start with a circle, a line, or a
star and see where it leads you . . .

What are you looking forward to this year?

JANUARY 2
EAT A GOOD BREAKFAST

What do you like to eat for breakfast?
A warm bowl of oatmeal on a chilly
winter's morning can taste just right.

You can sprinkle different kinds of
ingredients on top to make it special.
What do you want to add to your bowl today?

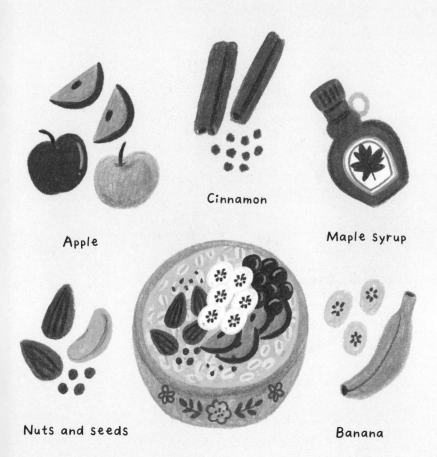

Apple

Cinnamon

Maple Syrup

Nuts and seeds

Banana

JANUARY 3
READ AND REST

It feels good to take it easy, especially
after a celebration.

So, get into your pajamas early, put on your
slippers, and cozy up with a good book.

Spend some of today reading and resting.
Sleep helps your body, mind, and memory
grow strong.

Where is your favorite place to rest and relax?
What makes it so special?

JANUARY 4
WORLD BRAILLE DAY

Louis Braille was born on this day in 1809. Louis lost his sight when he was three years old. When he got older, he created a code called braille so he could read. Braille is made up of raised dots. The dots are arranged in different patterns to represent letters and are read by touch.

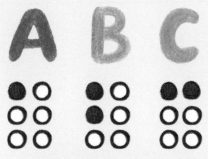

Today, braille is celebrated around the world. It continues to help millions of people with impaired vision read.

JANUARY 5
SPOT A BIRD

Birds are so important to our planet.
They spread seeds and pollinate flowers.
This helps other plants grow.

Birds are beautiful. What birds
do you see where you live?

Starling

House Sparrow

Woodpecker

Osprey

Peregrine
falcon

JANUARY 6
CUDDLE

Today, be thankful for cuddling.

Cuddle up with your stuffed animal.
Get cozy under a blanket,
read stories,
share secrets,
hug it tightly.

Do you have a favorite stuffed animal?
What's its name?

JANUARY 7
START A ROCK COLLECTION

Rocks are fascinating.

Did you know that some rocks were formed from volcanic eruptions?

Old rocks can also hold fossils, bits of animals and plants that lived a long, long time ago. These fossils help scientists learn about what life was like in the past.

Pick up a rock, hold it in your hand, and wonder. Where did it come from?

Start your own rock collection today.

JANUARY 8
MAKE A
BUBBLE BATH

Bubbles are joyful.
Add liquid soap to your
bath or a bucket of water,
lather up and play!

Can you make a bubble wig?
Scoop piles of bubbles together
and make a bubble sculpture.
Pour water into a mountain of
bubbles and watch them dissolve.

How do bubbles feel on your skin?

JANUARY 9
BUNDLE UP

Brrr! January can be a cold month.
Give thanks for all the things that keep
you warm and brighten your winter days.

Soft sweaters

Puffy coats

Gloves and
mittens

Fluffy earmuffs

Fuzzy socks

JANUARY 10
LOOK AFTER YOUR HOUSEPLANTS

Green things can make us happier, especially in the wintertime. Today is the perfect day to give your houseplants some extra love and care.

1. Check the soil. If it's dry, give your plant some water.

2. If you can, add a little fertilizer or plant food.

3. Remove any dead leaves.

4. Say thank you! Plants give you fresh air to breathe in every day.

JANUARY 11
MAKE A PLAYLIST

Make a list of your favorite songs today.

Songs from a favorite movie.
Songs that make you want to sing along.
Songs that make you want to play an instrument.
Songs that remind you of a special person, place, or time.

Put your songs together in a playlist.
What will you name it?

Listen to your playlist when you need a mood
boost or whenever you feel happy.

JANUARY 12
PLAY IN THE SNOW

There are SNOW many ways to play in winter.

What are your favorite things to do?

Zoom

Slide

Jump

Flap your wings

JANUARY 13
DESIGN A STICKER

R. Stanton Avery was born on this day in 1907.
He invented the sticker!

Design your own sticker.
Draw one on a piece of paper.
Color it and then cut it out.
Place it on to a piece of tape
to make it sticky.

Who can you give your sticker to?
Where can you stick a burst of joy?

JANUARY 14
DRESS UP YOUR PET

Pets do things every day that make us smile.
Take time to play with your pet today.
Have fun with accessories, costumes, or props.
You can even include your stuffed animals!
Draw a picture of your pet, or take a
photograph to hang on your bedroom wall.

JANUARY 15
TAKE ACTION LIKE
MARTIN LUTHER KING, JR.

Today is Martin Luther King, Jr.'s birthday.
He was a civil rights activist from Atlanta, Georgia,
who wanted black people to be treated equally.

He took action to help others, and he inspired
millions of people to help others, too.

Look for ways to take action today.
What does Martin Luther King, Jr. inspire you to do?

JANUARY 16
CREATE A MAGICAL CREATURE

Dragons are majestic, fire-breathing wonders!
Create your own magical creature today.
What special powers will it have?
What colors will it be?
What will you name it?

We can use our imagination
to create incredible things.

JANUARY 17
BECOME AN INVENTOR

To invent is to think up or create something for the first time.

When a boy named Chester Greenwood was ice-skating, he didn't like how his ears got cold. He asked his grandmother to sew tufts of fur between loops of wire. Together, they created the first pair of earmuffs.

When you face a problem today, take a moment to think how you could make it better. You might just end up inventing something!

JANUARY 18
SHARE YOUR FEELINGS

A thesaurus is terrific for finding words that mean similar things. We can find lots of words to describe how we're feeling.

Pick a word that describes how you feel today. See if you can find three other ways to describe it, too.

When we tell others how we're feeling, we can brighten their day or they can brighten ours.

Excited

Peppy

Grumpy

Bouncy

Crotchety

Calm

Relaxed

Peaceful

Crabby

JANUARY 19
COLLECT TREASURES

The beginning of the year is a good time
to start collecting things that bring you joy.

Find a box and stash little mementos
in it throughout the year.

In December, you'll enjoy the moments
these little treasures help you remember.

JANUARY 20
BUILD A FORT

Today is a great day to build a fort.
What kind of fort would you like to build?

You could build . . .
a snow fort,
a blanket fort,
a cardboard fort,
a secret fort,
a fort for friends,
or a fort just for you.

JANUARY 21
ASK FOR A HUG

Did you know that hugs have magic powers?
Hugs keep our hearts and minds
healthy and strong.

Ask for a hug today.
How does it make you feel?

A good hug can make you feel
like you can do anything.

JANUARY 22
GO ON A WINTER WALK

Go for a walk today and take in what's
happening in nature.

See a bird. A squirrel. An insect.
Listen to the wind. A bird chirping.
A car going by.
Touch a smooth rock. A rough tree trunk.
A dry leaf.

What things can you smell on your walk?
How does being outside make you feel?

JANUARY 23
WRITE A LETTER

Did you know that we all have
different handwriting?

Write to someone special today.
Address and stamp the envelope.
Stick it in the mail.

Whoever gets your letter will see your
handwriting and smile.

JANUARY 24
SHARE A LAUGH

Laughter is a burst of joy coming out of your body. A belly laugh is something that happens when you laugh so hard your belly hurts!

The next time something makes you laugh, share what it is with a friend and pass on the joy.

JANUARY 25
DO THE OPPOSITE

Add a little whimsy to your day.
Say goodbye instead of hello.
Brush your teeth with your other hand.
Wear your backpack on your front.
Talk about your day using all opposite words.
Tuck a parent into bed and read them a story!

JANUARY 26
PLAY A UKULELE

A ukulele is a stringed instrument
that looks like a small guitar.
It has a fun and cheerful sound.
Ukulele music is very popular around the
world, especially in Hawai'i.

Play or listen to some ukulele music today.
What does it make you think of?

JANUARY 27
PLAY WITH BUBBLE WRAP

Pop, pop, pop!
Sometimes the best part of a package is the bubble wrap.
It feels good to pop it, and it sounds good, too. Some people
like to pop one bubble at a time. Others like
to twist and pop them all at once.

What do you like to do with bubble wrap? Whatever you
decide to do, once you've finished playing with bubble
wrap, make sure you reuse or recycle it.

JANUARY 28
ADMIRE A TOWER

On this day in 1887, work on the Eiffel Tower began in Paris, France. It was completed in 1889 for the World's Fair, where some of the most advanced inventions and discoveries were showcased.

Today, it is one of the most recognizable structures in the world.

Look for unique buildings around you today. Which ones make you feel special or joyful?

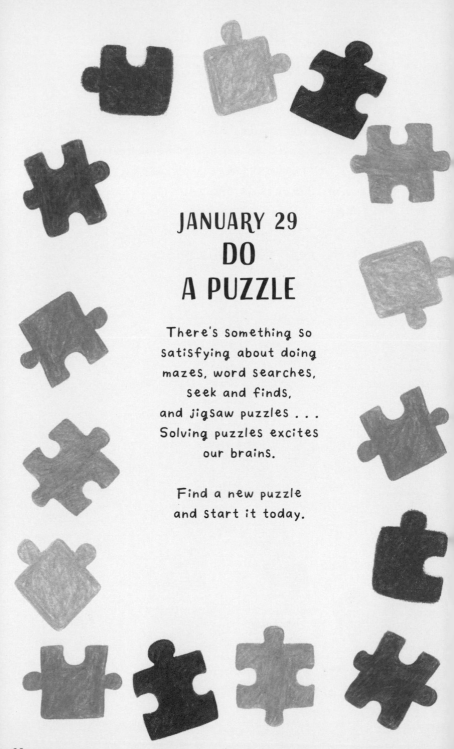

JANUARY 29
DO
A PUZZLE

There's something so
satisfying about doing
mazes, word searches,
seek and finds,
and jigsaw puzzles . . .
Solving puzzles excites
our brains.

Find a new puzzle
and start it today.

JANUARY 30
EAT A PASTRY

The story goes that these crescent-shaped treats were invented in Vienna, Austria. When an Austrian baker opened up a shop in Paris, France, in the 1800s, they became the pastries we know today as croissants: flaky on the outside and soft on the inside.

What type of pastry do you like to eat? Have one today, and try to slow down and savor every bite.

JANUARY 31
MAKE A TINY TOY WORLD

What do you like to play with every day?
Do you have special stuffed animals, figures, or dolls?

Spend some time today making a unique universe
for your toys.

Make furniture
out of paper and
cardboard.

Build a house
from a shoebox.

Act out scenes
in the places
you create.

Arrange little items
to make a store.

Sometimes it's so much fun to go into a world of pretend.

FEBRUARY 1
CELEBRATE TRADITION

Lunar New Year is a holiday celebrated all over the world. It's on a different date in January or February, depending on the lunar calendar.

People welcome and encourage a year filled with happiness, health, and prosperity with many traditions.

Oranges are lucky because of their bright color.
Firecrackers scare away bad spirits.
Dancing dragons symbolize great power.

What traditions do you celebrate?

FEBRUARY 2
READ ALOUD

In February each year, people around
the world celebrate reading aloud.

Pick a book to share with someone today.
Ask them, "Can you read this with me?"
Sharing stories is one of the best ways
to spend time with family and friends.

FEBRUARY 3
WEAR A FUN OUTFIT

Wear something today that
makes you feel happy.
Does it make you feel
anything else?

Fierce

Fast

Cozy

Comfortable

Sparkly

Cute

FEBRUARY 4
THANK POSTAL WORKERS

Postal workers bring us birthday cards, postcards, and packages. Wouldn't it be fun to deliver something to them? Stick a card on your mailbox to say, "Thank you!"

It'll send them on their way with a smile.

FEBRUARY 5
CELEBRATE WINTER

Winterlude is a festival celebrated in early February in Canada's Capital Region. It's a celebration of winter, featuring ice sculpture competitions, the world's largest ice-skating rink, an ice dragon boat race, and giant slides made of snow.

Think about how you like to play in winter and create your own winterlude activity today.

FEBRUARY 6
JUMP UP AND DOWN

Feeling a little blue from winter?
Try jumping!

On the sofa . . .

On a trampoline . . .

JUMP!

JUMP!

Off a
Snowbank!

FEBRUARY 7
SOLVE A PROBLEM

Have you ever heard the saying,
"Don't cry over spilled milk"?

People say it because everyone spills things or has small accidents. After all, that's what towels are for.

Sometimes, it helps to remember that most problems have solutions.

FEBRUARY 8
START A LIST

Think about the people you love. What makes them smile?
What makes them laugh? Start a list.

When it's their birthday, or just when you
want to surprise them, use your list to do
something extra nice for them.

FEBRUARY 9
READ IN THE BATH

Have you ever read in the bath?
Give it a try today!

Soak in a whole new world.
(Just keep a towel handy!)

FEBRUARY 10
BE GRATEFUL FOR UMBRELLAS

Today, appreciate one of the most useful inventions.
An umbrella can be a sprinkle of delight on a rainy day.

What kind of umbrella brings you joy?

Rainbow polka dots

Sunny yellow

Spiky dinosaur

Clear as a bubble

FEBRUARY 11
INTERNATIONAL DAY OF WOMEN AND GIRLS IN SCIENCE

On this day, people around the world celebrate the achievements of women and girls in science and technology. It's an important celebration because historically they have been underrepresented.

Think of a woman you know who works in science, maybe a doctor, teacher, or engineer.
The next time you see her, ask her questions.
"What do you like best about what you do?"

There are fascinating people all around us.

FEBRUARY 12
DISCOVER THE NIGHT SKY

Step outside and look up at the night sky.

What colors do you see?
What shines?
What twinkles?

Can you see the moon tonight?
What shape is it?

FEBRUARY 13
CHERISH A FRIEND

Isn't it special when you have someone
that likes the same things you like
and laughs at the same things that
make you laugh?

Can you think of three happy times
you've shared with a friend?

FEBRUARY 14
VALENTINE'S DAY

Today, people around the world express their affection with greetings and gifts. It is a lovely day for showing others that you care about them.

Use what you know about loved ones to do something nice. (You can use your list from February 8!) When you notice others, it helps them feel great.

Make a book and fill it with lovely things.

Make a snack they like.

Make a card to say something nice.

Make a bouquet of flowers.

FEBRUARY 15
ASK QUESTIONS LIKE GALILEO

Galileo was born on this day in 1564. He was a famous Italian scientist, mathematician, and astronomer who made fascinating discoveries. He was the first to see Saturn's rings and Jupiter's moons. Galileo asked a lot of questions and made up experiments to try and find the answers.

Celebrate Galileo today and look closely at the world around you. Ask yourself questions like: What if? Why? How come? Enjoy trying to figure out the answers.

FEBRUARY 16
CATCH A SNOWFLAKE

The next time it snows . . .
Tip your face up to the sky,
close your eyes, and
stretch out your tongue.
What does a snowflake taste like?

FEBRUARY 17
BE KIND

Being kind feels good.

Give a compliment.

Offer a hug.

Lend a hand.

FEBRUARY 18
DISCOVER SOMETHING NEW

The dwarf planet Pluto was discovered in 1930.
It was named by an 11-year-old girl named
Venetia Burney of Oxford, England.

Today, see if you can discover something
you've never seen before.
It doesn't have to be as big as Pluto.
Little discoveries are fun, too.

FEBRUARY 19
LEARN ABOUT INVENTIONS

In 1878, Thomas Edison patented the phonograph. This sound recording device went on to inform many of the machines that we still use today, like the telephone.

Take a look around your home today.
What gadgets or devices bring you joy?

FEBRUARY 20
WORLD DAY OF
SOCIAL JUSTICE

Social justice is the belief that all people should have the same rights, like access to clean air and water, healthy food, and safe spaces.

Today, people around the world are fighting to achieve equal rights.

Look for ways you can help make your community more fair, more equal, and more joyful for all.

FEBRUARY 21
CURL UP AND CLIMB

World Pangolin Day falls in February each year.
Pangolins live in a variety of habitats in Africa and Asia.

Their name comes from a Malaysian word that means
"to roll over." When they get scared, they roll into a
tight ball.

Does this happen to you, too?
It's OK. You're just having a
pangolin moment. And when you feel
ready to climb tall trees, that's
a pangolin moment, too.

FEBRUARY 22
ENJOY WINTER YOGA

Today, move through these wintry yoga poses.

Winter rainbow

Sledding hill

Snowy mountain

Downhill skier

Hibernating bear

FEBRUARY 23
MAKE A BRACELET

Make a beautiful beaded bracelet today.
String bright beads on a pipe cleaner or a piece
of string. Wear it for some colorful cheer.

Or, why not give it to someone to brighten their day?

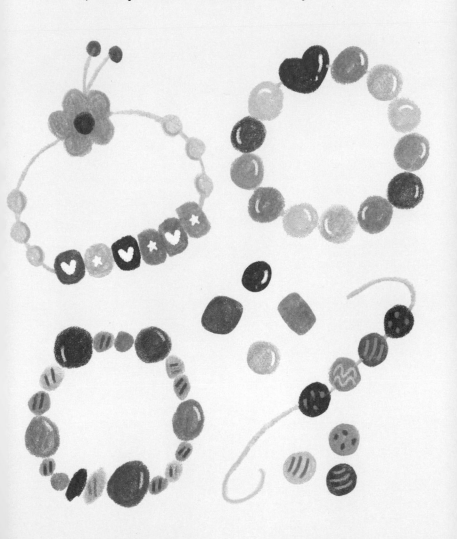

FEBRUARY 24
EAT TORTILLA CHIPS

Crunch, crunch, crunch!
There are so many ways to eat tortilla chips.

Salsa

Beans

Guacamole

Cheese

Peppers

Olives

How do you like to eat them?

FEBRUARY 25
PLAY A CARD GAME

You can play something simple
or something elaborate.
You can play with a big group,
with one person,
or by yourself.

What are your favorite card games?

FEBRUARY 26
MAKE UP A STORY

Read a fairy tale or create your own
story to share with someone today.

What is the story about?
Who is in the story?
Where does the story take place?

Making up stories is a special kind of magic.

FEBRUARY 27
HELP POLAR BEARS

Climate change is hurting polar bears. Their homes
on the ice caps are melting. But you can help today.

Unplug electronics when you're not using them to save
energy. Using less energy is good for the ice
caps and good for polar bears.

There are a lot of little things we can all
do to help these beautiful animals.

FEBRUARY 28
PLAY THE DRUMS

There are different kinds of drums all over the world. Some drums you play with your hands and some with sticks.

The djembe is a West African hand drum. It can make different kinds of sounds depending on what part of your hand you use and where on the drum face you strike it. When you beat it in the middle with your palm, it makes a low sound. It makes a higher sound when you tap the edges with your fingers.

Play the drums today, or experiment with tapping out different rhythms on things you have around the house.

FEBRUARY 29
LEAP DAY

A leap day is added to the calendar during leap years, which happen every four years.

A leap is a big, long jump.
So, jump into a big idea today.
Plan to do something that is giant to you.

Start to read an epic book.

Paint a huge picture.

Tackle a new hobby.

Run a long distance.

Today is a day for the extraordinary!

MARCH 1
GIVE A COMPLIMENT

A compliment is a way of saying what you like about someone or naming something they do well.

It's like a hug or a high five with words.
Try giving three people a compliment today.
Then see how you feel!

That was an awesome goal!

You're a thoughtful friend.

I'd like to be able to cook like you!

You're a great listener.

You tell funny stories.

MARCH 2
CELEBRATE A BIRTHDAY

Every day is somebody's birthday.

Around the world, people celebrate birthdays in different ways. In the Philippines, people eat long noodles to symbolize good luck for a long life.

Do you know anyone who is celebrating a birthday today? What could you do to wish them a happy year ahead?

MARCH 3
WORLD WILDLIFE DAY

Today, people celebrate all the different
wild animals and plants on our planet.

Elephants in
the grasslands

Toucans
in the
rainforest

Leopards in the jungle

Narwhals in the
Arctic waters

Koalas in
the forests

When we appreciate our planet,
we can work to protect it.

MARCH 4
MAKE A SCRAPBOOK

Make a scrapbook to bring you cheer today and in the future.

1. Find mementos such as photographs, ticket stubs, cards, or stickers that remind you of a special place, time, or trip.

2. Arrange your bits and pieces.

3. Use glue or decorative tape to stick items to the page.

4. Write down stories and descriptions next to each item.

On the next rainy day, you can look through your scrapbook and see all your fun memories.

MARCH 5
SHARE A BOOK

Share some of your favorite books today.

You can write a letter to a family member or a friend today and suggest a book that they might like. Then, why not ask them to recommend a book for you?

MARCH 6
CELEBRATE YOUR SMILE

Show a little love to your teeth today.
Without them, we couldn't chew
the food we love to eat.

Pay extra attention while you're brushing your teeth.
Floss and rinse, too.
A healthy smile feels fresh and clean.

MARCH 7
GET PLANT POWER

When we eat food, we get the nutrients we need to live.
Food gives us energy and power.

Take some time today to notice the variety
of foods we get from plants.

What new plant-based foods would you like to try?

Hummus with
vegetable sticks

Bread and
jam

Vegetable curry
and rice

Fruit platter

Mushroom, tomato,
and broccoli pizza

MARCH 8
INTERNATIONAL WOMEN'S DAY

This day, recognized in countries all over the world,
brings attention to women's achievements and
the need for equal rights.

In Italy, people celebrate by giving women
bright yellow mimosa flowers.

What could you do today to thank the
women in your life for all they do?

MARCH 9
TAKE A SIESTA

In Spain, shops close for a few hours in the afternoon. This gives people time to take a long lunch, rest, and stay out of the hot midday sun. This is known as a siesta.

What can you do to slow down and enjoy your afternoon today?

MARCH 10
INTERNATIONAL BAGPIPE DAY

Today, people are celebrating bagpipes around the world.
Bagpipes are ancient instruments that have been played
for centuries in parts of Europe, Asia, and Africa.

Bagpipes make a strong, loud sound.
The music from bagpipes can fill a big space.

There are many different varieties,
and each plays a distinct sound.

Listen to some bagpipe music today.
How would you describe it?

MARCH 11
EXPLORE YOUR NAME

Uncover the history of your name today.
Ask your family questions.

Where did the idea for your name come from?
Were you named after someone in the family?
Were you named after a famous person or place?

There are always interesting things
we can learn about ourselves.

MARCH 12
PLANT A FLOWER

Spring is just around the corner!
Prepare for the change of season today.

Plant a flower, indoors or outside.

Place a few fresh flowers on your table.

Move your houseplant to a new spot in the sun.

Give flowers to family or friends to make them smile.

January
garnet

February
amethyst

March
aquamarine

December
tanzanite

MARCH 13
DISCOVER YOUR
BIRTHSTONE

April
diamond

Most gemstones come from
the Earth. Do you know
your birthstone?

November
citrine

What do these gemstones
make you think of?
Jewelry?
Treasure?
Magic?

May
emerald

What special powers
might they hold?

October
opal

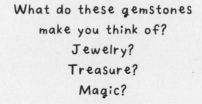

June
pearl

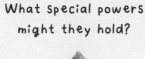
August
peridot

July
ruby

September
sapphire

MARCH 14
PI DAY

Today is known around the world as Pi Day.

Pi is equal to the ratio of a circle's circumference (how big it is around) to its diameter (the distance across the circle's center). No matter how big or small a circle, the ratio is always the same!

People celebrate pi by . . . eating pie. Yum!
Experiment and play with pi today.
Measure plates, lids, wheels, and hula hoops.

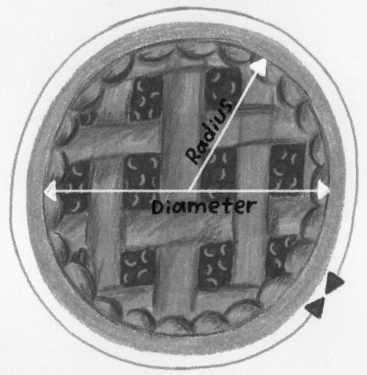

Circumference

Radius

Diameter

MARCH 15
USE YOUR VOICE

On this day in 2019, more than one million school children around the world participated in climate change strikes.

They were inspired by Greta Thunberg who, at age 15, protested all by herself outside the Swedish parliament. She called on her government to make changes that would be better for the planet. Her voice led to millions of voices bringing attention to the Earth.

Are there things in the world that you think need to change?

Use your voice today. Others will listen.

MARCH 16
FIND NICE SMELLS

Think of three things that smell nice today.
What are they?
What do they smell like?
What do they make you think of?

Lemon

Vanilla

Apples and
cinnamon

Lavender

Chocolate chip
cookies

Grass

Crayons

Snow

MARCH 17
SAINT PATRICK'S DAY

Bring out your green! On this day each year, people from all around the world celebrate Irish culture. The day is packed with parades, good luck charms, and all things green.

Which of these lucky things can you find today?

Rainbow

Horseshoe

Gold coins

Evidence of a leprechaun

Shamrocks

Green food

MARCH 18
LEARN ABOUT GUIDE DOGS

Guide dogs are specially trained animals.
They help many blind and partially sighted people
travel around safely.

Learn about guide dogs today
and the hard work that they do.

It's wonderful that these animals are in our world.

MARCH 19
SAY GOODBYE TO WINTER

Around this time of year, the spring equinox is approaching. Have a closing ceremony to mark the end of winter.

Make some hot chocolate, wrap up in a blanket, and think about the things that you enjoyed this season.

What do you love about wintertime?

I love taking out my favorite Christmas ornaments and choosing just the right spot for them on the Christmas tree.

Throwing snowballs with my friends made me laugh so hard.

I felt cozy and snug wearing warm, fuzzy socks.

I watched fluffy snowflakes fall and caught them on my tongue.

MARCH 20
INTERNATIONAL DAY
OF HAPPINESS

Around the world today, people are celebrating happiness.
Making someone happy can make you happy, too.

If you can make one person smile, then they can make
a second person smile. And then a third person, too.
A smile can spread across the whole world.

How could you make someone smile today?
Try slipping cheerful notes into places for people to find.

You might be surprised how simple things
can spread joy.

MARCH 21
SAY YOUR FAVORITE WORD

Finding the perfect word to describe
something can feel like any of these things!

Triumphant

Joyful

Blissful

Glorious

Awesome

Exhilarating

Euphoric

What is your favorite word?
Say it out loud. How does it make you feel?

MARCH 22
WORLD WATER DAY

Today, people across the globe focus on the
importance of fresh water.

Water is amazing!

For washing, drinking,
splashing, sprinkling.

For warm baths.
For icy drinks.

For puddles.
For giving us life.

Take a moment to be thankful for fresh water today.

MARCH 23
GREET THE BLOSSOMS

Look up! Look down! Spring symbolizes new life.

Did you know that different kinds
of plants bloom at different times?

Flowering cherry

Forsythia

Flowering
magnolias

Crocuses

Hyacinths

Irises

Daffodils

Pansies

Tulips

What do you notice in spring where you live?

MARCH 24
DRAW A MAP

How well do you know where you live?
Draw a map of your bedroom, home, town, or city.

Where are the special places?
What makes them special to you?

LIBRARY

PARK

HOME ♥

OLIVER'S HOME

TREASURE

FAVORITE PLACE

ICE CREAM SHOP!

MARCH 25
MOVE YOUR BODY

Moving our bodies can help us feel happy and strong.

Grab a piece of paper, a pencil, and two dice,
and play a movement game today.

1. Number a piece of paper 1 through 6.

2. Write down a physical activity next to each number.

3. Roll the first dice. The number you roll will tell
   you which activity to do.

4. Roll the second dice. The number you roll will tell
   you how many of each activity to do.

Sit-ups

Jumping jacks

Hop on one
foot

MARVEL AT BUTTERFLIES

Keep an eye out for beautiful butterflies.
The butterflies on this page are common in early spring.

Go outside today.
What butterflies can you find?

Tiger
swallowtail

Orange tip

Peacock

Mourning cloak

Monarch

MARCH 27
WORLD THEATER DAY

Today, going to the theater to see shows
is celebrated worldwide.

It's fun to be together with a big crowd to . . .
laugh out loud,
jump in fright,
hold your breath in suspense.

Have you ever seen a show in a theater?
Would you rather be in the audience,
working behind the scenes, or on the stage?

MARCH 28
WELCOME WEEDS

What do you think about weeds?

Most people think of weeds as a nuisance.
But, did you know that dandelions are weeds?

These pops of yellow signal the start of spring.
Dandelions can push themselves up between stones
and cracks in the pavement. When the petals change
into a puffball of seeds, they can carry wishes.

If you find a dandelion today, what will you wish for?

MARCH 29
WORLD PIANO DAY

Each year, a global event takes place on the 88th day. It honors the piano and its 88 keys!

Pianos are unique instruments.
They have strings like violins and guitars.
They are also percussion instruments like drums.
When you play keys on a piano, you're making little hammers bang on strings.

Pianos have a versatile sound. They can sound light and happy to sad and spooky.

Try to pick out the sounds of a piano in the songs you hear today.

MARCH 30
USE A PENCIL

A pencil is a great tool for writing or drawing.
Think about how satisfying it can be to use a pencil.

You can doodle,
design, and sketch.

They have
erasers.

They feel good
in your hand.

They're fun
to sharpen.

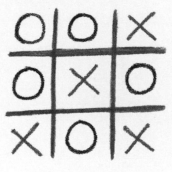

You can play.

They come in a
rainbow of colors.

MARCH 31
DO A SPRING CLEAN

Look for trash when you're outside today.

Pick up wrappers, bags, and papers
and toss them in the trash can.

Recycle anything that you can.

Wash your hands when you're done.

You just helped make the world a little better.

Tell your friends about it to inspire
them to pick up trash, too.

APRIL 1
PLAN A PRANK

Today is the day for playful mischief
in many countries around the world.

The French have a tradition called "Poisson d'Avril"
or "April fish." You tape a paper fish to someone's
back without them knowing!

Pick someone who would enjoy an April Fools'
joke and plan a prank for them today.

APRIL 2
AUTISM AWARENESS DAY

We all need air to breathe.
We all need food and water.
We all need to connect with others.

Autism affects how the brain works. Someone with autism
may see, hear, and feel the world differently than
someone without autism. Someone with autism might find it
hard to know what others are feeling without being told,
or to make eye contact when they're talking or listening.
But, that doesn't mean they don't want to connect.

Here are some ways to make anyone feel
comfortable and welcome.

Give them your
attention.

What is
your favorite
food?

wow!
You draw
so well!

Ask a friendly
question.

Wave hello.

APRIL 3
EXPRESS GRATITUDE

For Muslim people, Ramadan is a holy time dedicated to gratitude and giving. It lasts one month and its dates are based on the lunar calendar. During Ramadam, Muslims do not eat between sunrise and sunset, and they accept the feelings of hunger to remind them to be grateful for food and other good things in their lives. They are encouraged to help the poor, hungry, and homeless by giving food and donating money.

Take time today to be thankful for the food you eat. Is there a way you can help out a local food bank or charity?

APRIL 4
EAT YOUR VITAMINS

Vitamin C is so good for our bodies.
It helps our immune system, which helps us fight germs.
It keeps our skin, bones, and teeth healthy.
And do you know what's even better?
Vitamin C is in lots of tasty foods.

Melons

Kiwis

Strawberries

Guavas

Broccoli

Sweet yellow
peppers

Kale

Oranges

What vitamin-rich foods can
you find in your home today?

APRIL 5
ENJOY A POEM

Painters create with paint.
Musicians create with instruments.
Poets create with words.
They choose words for their
meaning, sound and rhythm.

Today . . .
Read a poem,
love a poem,
write a poem,
share a poem.

APRIL 6
DISCOVER YOUR NATIONAL FLOWER

Cherry blossoms, or sakura, are
the national flower of Japan.

When the wind blows, pink petals fall like rain.

These flowers bloom for a short time and remind
us to slow down and take in their beauty.

What is the national flower where you live?

WRITE A HAIKU

A haiku is a short form of Japanese poetry.
It tries to capture the essence or beauty
of something in three short lines.

The first line is five syllables.
The second line is seven syllables.
The third line is five syllables.

I like collecting.
Rocks, gems, jewels, gold, fortune.
Treasure surrounds us.

Try writing your own haiku today.

APRIL 8
BE BOLD LIKE
TINY BROADWICK

Georgia Broadwick was given the nickname "Tiny"
when she was born weighing only 2 pounds.
When she grew up, she was about 5 feet tall and
weighed less than 88 pounds. But that didn't
stop her from accomplishing daring feats.

Tiny parachuted out of hot-air balloons and became the
first woman to parachute out of an airplane.

She proved that you can be bold, courageous,
mighty . . . and tiny.

APRIL 9
IMAGINE A UNICORN

What would you do if you met a unicorn today?

It's great to imagine these magical, majestic creatures in the world. Whether they exist or not, the thought of unicorns can make us happy.

APRIL 10
FIND SIMPLE FIXES

Safety pins are so small and simple,
but they can solve all kinds of problems.

They fix things.

They secure things.

They replace things.

They keep things together.

They make things pretty.

What is something really simple that solves
a problem or makes your day easier?

APRIL 11
GROW A PLANT

To be amazed a little every day, watch plants grow.

Plant a window box.

Plant herbs.

Plant a seed in a little pot.

Plant a garden.

What would you like to grow today?

APRIL 12
WALK ON YOUR WILD SIDE

Let yourself go wacky and wild today.
Show enthusiasm for something you like.

Wear things that make you feel excited.
Do something fun with your hair.
Be unpredictable.

Others might think you are a bit too wild.
Or they might want to join in!

APRIL 13
PLAY A BOARD GAME

In 1929, many people in the United States were facing tough times. They were out of work and had very little money for food. Alfred Mosher Butts wanted people to have fun, so, in 1933, he invented the board game that would eventually become Scrabble.

This simple word game with small lettered tiles has provided fun for millions of people for almost 100 years.

What board games do you like to play?

SPEND TIME WITH FAMILY

Dolphins are delightful animals
and bring joy to our planet.

They live in big groups called pods and travel
by swimming and leaping out of the water.

Dolphins in a pod play, help, and protect one another.

These animals move between different pods
throughout their lives.

Who is in your pod of family members?
What do you like to do together?

APRIL 15
KEEP A NOTEBOOK LIKE LEONARDO DA VINCI

On this day in 1452, Leonardo da Vinci was born.
He has been famous for more than 500 years!

Leonardo was a great artist and inventor who loved to
study nature, buildings, and the human body. He filled
notebooks with sketches, questions, and ideas.

Start writing in a notebook today, and jot down
your questions, ideas, and interests.

You can come up with great works,
just like Leonardo da Vinci.

APRIL 16
SHARE A HIGH FIVE

Today, celebrate the art of the high five.

A high five is a gesture of celebration in which
two people gently slap one another's palms
with their arms raised.

It is a simple and cheerful way to celebrate
accomplishments both big and small.

How many times can you high five today?

APRIL 17
CELEBRATE NEW LIFE

Easter is a Christian holiday that takes place in the spring. People in countries that celebrate Easter have different traditions.

In Italy, people bake "Pane di Pasqua," or "Easter bread." It's made by braiding three pieces of dough into a crown shape, tucking in colored eggs and baking it into a light and fluffy treat.

Eggs symbolize new life. Easter can remind us that we are loved, that our mistakes can be forgiven, and that we can begin each new day with a fresh start.

What are ways you can show love?
What are ways you can show forgiveness?

APRIL 18
HIT A PIÑATA

These colorful and creative candy containers are popular in celebrations and birthdays all over the world.

What do you like about a piñata?

The fun shapes?
Hitting them until they burst open?
The sweets and surprises?

What kind of piñata would you enjoy?
What would you like to be inside?

APRIL 19
TAKE CARE OF YOUR CLOTHES

Something's in the air . . .
the sweet smell of clean laundry.
Today, think about how we can take care
of our clothes to help the environment.

Hang laundry to dry
instead of using
a dryer to save
electricity.

Treat clothes gently
so that they last
longer and don't have
to be thrown away.

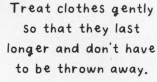

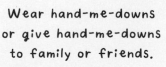

Wear hand-me-downs
or give hand-me-downs
to family or friends.

APRIL 20
LEARN CHINESE

More than one billion people speak Chinese.
More people speak Chinese as their first language
than any other language in the world!

Try learning or teaching someone a little Chinese today.
The more languages you know, the more people
you can talk to, learn from and have fun with.

你好

Hello

Nǐ hǎo (*Nee how*)

谢谢

Thank you

Xièxiè (*Shieh-shieh*)

别客气

You're welcome

Bié kèqì (*Boo kuh-chi*)

早上好

Good morning

Zǎo shàng hǎo (*Zhow shang how*)

APRIL 21
WORLD CREATIVITY AND INNOVATION DAY

On this day across the globe, people give attention to the importance of creativity and innovation.

Look for ideas for creating something brand new or think about how you could make existing things better.

Write down your ideas. Then, see if you can take the next step and make your ideas happen.

MY AWESOME TOASTER!

Can you improve your morning routine?
How can your school do something better?
What needs to be fixed in your town or city?

APRIL 22
EARTH DAY

Each Earth Day, people around the world participate in action to work toward a healthier environment.

Earth provides the air we breathe, the food we eat, the clothes we wear, and the homes we live in. Earth gives us mountains, oceans, and forests.

Take a deep breath in and let it out slowly . . . Think about and appreciate our planet today.

APRIL 23
DESIGN STATIONERY

Stationery is paper and envelopes made for writing letters.

When people receive letters in the mail, it shows that someone took extra time and care to send them a message.

Design your own stationery today and send a friend a letter. Are there colors that they might enjoy? Are there patterns that will remind your friend of you?

APRIL 24
SAVE MONEY

Saving money little by little can be really fun.

Today, start to put coins in a piggy bank
and watch your money grow.

Use the money you save to do something special
for yourself or for someone you care about.

Could you use your money to donate to a cause that's
important to you? Helping others can make you happy.

APRIL 25
SCAT SING LIKE ELLA FITZGERALD

On this day in 1917, Ella Fitzgerald was born. Ella was known as the Queen of Jazz. She had an amazing voice and could sing very low notes and very high notes.

Ella was famous for scat singing which is singing made-up sounds or nonsense words in a rhythmic way.

Listen to Ella today. How does her music make you feel?

Give scat singing a try. It's a fun way to sing and you don't have to know any words!

APRIL 26
GET ORGANIZED

Getting organized can give you a much-needed boost of energy!

What items do you like to use every day? Organize them neatly today, then look at them.

How do you feel now?

APRIL 27
LEARN MORSE CODE

Morse code is a type of code that is used to send telegraphic information using rhythm. It uses dots and dashes to show the letters of a given message.

Try learning a little Morse code today.
Then, teach it to a friend so they can understand, too.

You can communicate your secret code by writing notes, sending voice messages, or using a flashlight.

Communicating with friends can help us feel closer to each other.

APRIL 28
BE A SUPERHERO

Challenge yourself to be the best superhero today!

You can save the day in all kinds of ways.

Save an animal.
Save a classmate.

Save a friend.
Save a grown-up.

It's great to have heroes and to be a hero to others.

DANCE TO THE BEAT

Some days we can feel flat.
And other days we can feel excited.

Whatever we feel, we can put on
some music and move.

We can sway.
We can spin.
We can kick.
We can dance!

Today is International Dance Day, a global celebration
of dance, so put on some music and move.

INTERNATIONAL JAZZ DAY

Jazz is recognized as more than a type of music.
Jazz can bring people together, encourage expression,
and create opportunities to connect with one another.

Special jazz events are put on to unite people
in all corners of the globe on this day every year.
Today, you could . . .

Research famous
jazz musicians.

Dance to
different jazz
songs.

Listen to jazz while drawing
or painting a picture.

Watch videos
of jazz
performances.

You could invite a friend over to listen
or dance with you!

MAY 1
LOOK UP TO SPACE

Experience the mysteries of space today.
Look up at the sky, then close your eyes.

Imagine zooming above Earth . . .
Orbiting around the Sun . . .
Zipping around the planets in our solar system.

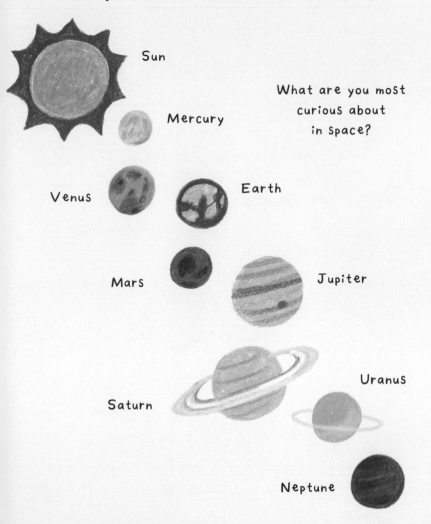

Sun

Mercury

Venus

Earth

Mars

Jupiter

Saturn

Uranus

Neptune

What are you most
curious about
in space?

MAY 2
RIDE YOUR BIKE

Bike riding is good for you because it:
Builds strong muscles including your heart.
Doesn't pollute the environment.
Helps you improve your balance.
Is a fun way to get from place to place!

Would you like to ride a bike solo or with a friend today?

MAY 3
TAKE A PHOTOGRAPH

Look at things from different points
of view and you'll find surprises.

Today, pick something to photograph:
Someone you love.
Something outside.
Something inside.
Something in the morning.
Something at night.

Take a picture of it:
Far away.
Up high.
Down low.
In light.
In shadow.

You can change how you see the world around you.

MAY 4
INTERNATIONAL FIREFIGHTERS' DAY

Today, people all around the world come together to thank firefighters. Firefighters protect our homes, our communities, and the natural land around us.

To show your gratitude for their hard work, wear a red and blue ribbon: red for fire and blue for water.

You could also visit your local fire station and say thank you.

There are people who work to keep us safe every day.

MAY 5
ENJOY SPRING YOGA

So many things are in bloom in the spring.

Celebrate growing things today as you move
through these spring yoga poses.

Flower pose

Spring rain

Flying butterfly

MAY 6
QUENCH YOUR THIRST

There's nothing more refreshing than a cold glass
of water, but it's nice to have a little variety.

What are some of your favorite things to drink?
When do you like to drink them?

Hot
chocolate

Lemonade

Milk

Apple juice

Coconut water

Smoothie

MAY 7
BLOW BUBBLES

Blowing bubbles can lift your spirits.

Today, make your own bubbles. You'll need:
- 3 tablespoons dish soap
- 1 cup water

1. Measure the dish soap into a container.

2. Slowly add in the water. Gently stir the mixture.

3. If you can, let the bubble mixture rest before using it.

Look for different items around your house that can be used to make a bubble wand. How about a straw, a cookie cutter, or a pipe cleaner?

When you're ready, dip your bubble wand into the mixture. Take a deep breath and gently blow a bubble.

How many bubbles can you make?

MAY 8
FREE YOUR FEET

Take off your socks and let your feet breathe today.

Wiggle your toes in the grass or on a fluffy rug.

Scrunch your toes tight, then stretch them out wide.

Flex and point your feet.

Move them in inside circles and outside circles.

Applaud your feet by clapping them together.

Yay for feet!

MAY 9
BELLY DANCE

Belly dancing is a type of dance that is popular in the Middle East. Give it a try today.

Stand with your back straight and your knees bent.

Straighten your right leg and lift up your right hip.

Switch to straighten your left leg and lift your left hip.

Alternate sides a little faster.

Put on some music and try out your new moves. How else do you like to move to music?

MAY 10
WONDER ABOUT WINDMILLS

Windmills were originally invented to grind grain in Iran. Later, they were used to pump water.

Check out the history of windmills and how they're helping us today.

Modern windmills can be found all over the world producing electricity.

If you live in an area that has a windmill, go out and watch it turn, turn, turn . . .

MAY 11
TIDY UP

A clean space can make us feel calm, energized,
confident, and happy. Have a look around your room
today. Is there an area that you can tidy up?
Go through your toys, books, knick-knacks, or artwork.

What do you want to save?
What can you donate to give someone else joy?
What can you clear away to make room for
more joy in your own space?

MAY 12
INTERNATIONAL NURSES DAY

Nurses are essential in every community.
They work hard in hospitals, schools, and homes
to keep people healthy and safe.

Nurses take good care of us.
Today, we can take care of them!

Thank some of the nurses in your life.
Make them a card or a sign. It would mean
so much and really make their day.

Your card or sign could say . . .

You are a
lifesaver!

Best nurse
ever!

You make a
difference!

Thank you for
taking good
care of us!

Nurses are
superheroes!

MAY 13
HAVE SOME HUMMUS

Hummus is a Middle Eastern and Mediterranean dish.
It comes from the Arabic word for chickpeas
because it is made from cooked and mashed chickpeas,
blended with other flavors like tahini, olive oil,
lemon juice, salt, or garlic.

Have you ever eaten hummus?
If not, why don't you give it a try?

You can discover delicious foods by trying something
new or eating familiar foods in new ways.

MAY 14
MAKE A MAGIC WAND

A woodland walk is even better with a magic wand.
Make your own today.

Take some ribbon or colored thread and hunt
for the most interesting stick.
Collect other natural items like feathers,
fallen leaves, and flowers.
Decorate your stick by wrapping your ribbon
or colored thread around it.
Tuck in and tie to your wand the
other treasures you've found.

When your wand is finished, hold it in your
hands, close your eyes, and chant a spell.

We can create magic using everyday things.

MAY 15
THROW A PIZZA PARTY

In Iceland, a common pizza topping is . . . banana!

Invent your own pizza today.
Pick a base, a sauce, and a topping.

Will you pick familiar foods?
Or try a combination of something new?

Who would you invite to your pizza party?

MAY 16
SAVOR A STRAWBERRY

Red, heart-shaped, and covered with small seeds, strawberries are one of the most popular fruits in the world. They are in season from May through to September.

Eat a strawberry today and savor each bite.

Notice the texture...
Is it smooth?
Is it bumpy?

Notice the
scent...
Is it fresh?

Notice the flavor...
Is it sweet?
Is it sour?

Slowing down is an easy way to get more joy from what we eat.

MAY 17
CELEBRATE ALL KINDS OF LOVE

Celebrate the power of love today.
Love can be between all kinds of people.
Love can make all kinds of families.

Take a moment to think about the people who
fill up your heart with joy and happiness.

When we love and accept one another,
the world is a beautiful place.

MAY 18
VISIT A MUSEUM

Museums are spectacular places to explore.

There are all kinds of museums, from art and science to math and history. There are even museums for ice cream!

Plan a visit to a museum, either in person or virtually. Ask yourself . . .

What exhibit would I like to show a friend?

How did it make me feel?

What do I like about this museum?

Which exhibit will I remember most?

MAY 19
SOAK UP THE SUN

Did you know that the sun provides Vitamin D?
Vitamin D is a nutrient that helps strengthen bones
and teeth and helps our bodies fight diseases.

So, get outside today and enjoy the sun.
It's not a problem if the sun isn't shining. The
sun's rays can get through clouds, fog, and mist.

Spending time outside feels good in so many ways.
What do you like to do outside?

MAY 20
WORLD BEE DAY

On this day in 1734, Anton Janša, the pioneer of beekeeping was born. Today, people around the world acknowledge the important role of bees and beekeeping.

These busy little bees work hard to spread pollen, which helps plants grow.

We can protect bees by . . .

Buying local honey.

Supporting beekeepers.

Planting flowers that make nectar.

HONEY

MAY 21
RECORD YOUR THOUGHTS

Notebooks are treasure chests for your thoughts,
memories, and ideas.

You can jot things down when you:
Visit a new place.
Make up a new joke.
Feel big feelings.
Think of someone far away.
Spot something growing.
Doodle and daydream.

MAY 22
THINK LIKE SHERLOCK HOLMES

Sir Arthur Conan Doyle wrote mystery books
starring a detective named Sherlock Holmes.
Sherlock Holmes solved mysteries that no one
else could by paying close attention to details.

Pay close attention to your world today.
Note new sights, new sounds, new smells,
new people, new emotions, new experiences.

Who knows when these details might come in handy?

Some people love the suspense, excitement, and
satisfaction of reading a good mystery.
Do you?

MAY 23
FIND A COIN

Find a penny, pick it up, all day long you'll have good luck!

Coins have a long history of bringing luck.
See if you can spot coins while going about your day.

The more you look for signs of good fortune,
the more you'll find.

MAY 24
MAKE YOUR BROTHER SMILE

Do you have a brother or someone who is like a brother to you? Today is a great day to let them know how much they mean to you.

What do you like to do together?
What makes your brother laugh?
How does your brother make you laugh?

Give your brother a big hug today,
and see if you can make each other smile.

MAY 25
TAP DANCE

Tap dancing is a special type of dancing that makes sound.

Tap shoes have metal plates on the heel and toe areas. When dancers move their feet, they make rhythmic tapping sounds.

Today, put on your favorite music and a pair of shoes. Play around with tapping your feet to the rhythm of the music.

MAY 26
EXPERIMENT WITH FLIGHT

Experiment with paper planes today.
Try using paper in various sizes.
Investigate different ways to fold the wings.
Discover a design for a truly speedy flyer.

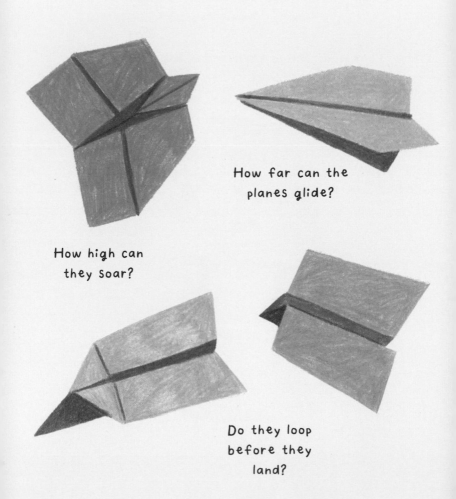

How far can the
planes glide?

How high can
they soar?

Do they loop
before they
land?

You can feed your curiosity with a few pieces of paper.

MAY 27
CELEBRATE COLOR

The Golden Gate Bridge in San Francisco opened on this day in 1937. Its famous color is known as international orange. The bright color helps the bridge stay visible in the fog and looks pleasing against the blue skies and green hills.

What colors do you find pleasing?
Celebrate the joy they bring today.

MAKE A SNACK TO SHARE

It feels good to surprise someone you care about, and it's simple, too!

Pick out some yummy foods.

Arrange them nicely on a plate.

Surprise, share, and smile!

MAY 29
USE A COMPOST

Home composting is one of the most environmentally friendly ways of dealing with food scraps.

Find out how you can compost in your community today.

5. Compost helps "feed" soil, which helps plants grow.

1. We eat yummy foods, like juicy red apples.

4. The food scraps break down into compost.

3. We throw them into a compost bin.

2. We don't throw food scraps into the trash.

All the things we do to help our Earth add up and can change the world.

MAY 30
PLAY WITH A BALL

You can have a lot of fun with a ball.

With friends or by yourself.
With a field of space or just a square.
With a hoop, a net, a hole, or a bat.

Sometimes the best games are the simplest.

MAY 31
FEEL A SENSE OF CALM

Start your day with a soothing morning ritual.

Sit on the floor with your legs crossed and eyes closed.

Take a slow, deep breath in through your nose
and release out through your mouth.

Continue to breathe in and out until you feel calm.

Slow, deep breaths carry oxygen to our brain.
This makes our brain and body feel better
so we can enjoy exactly where we are.

JUNE 1
GO CAMPING

Spend time in the great outdoors today.

Cooking by the fire, exploring nature, and sleeping under the stars are experiences to remember.

Play with making a tent at home or in your garden. Bring a snack and a friend.

JUNE 2
RUN FOR FUN

Ready, set, go!

When we run up a steep hill, through an open field,
while playing a sport, or racing against a friend,
we release good chemicals in our brain.

We are full of energy.
We feel strong.

What makes you feel strong?

JUNE 3
LISTEN TO AN AUDIOBOOK

Listening to a book being read aloud can
be relaxing or exciting.

Have you ever listened to an audiobook?
When do you like to relax with a book?

JUNE 4
HUG YOUR PET

Pets are important members of our families.
Share a snuggle with your dog, cat, rabbit,
or treasured stuffed animal today.
Enjoy feeling comfortable and content.

JUNE 5
WORLD ENVIRONMENT DAY

On this day, people all over the world take time to think about our environment and our planet.

Today, think about what you can do to conserve water.

Don't waste food. It takes a lot of water to grow fruit and vegetables!

Turn off the tap while you brush your teeth.

Use reusable water bottles.

Use the hose less and collect rain water instead.

When we take care of the Earth, the Earth can take care of us.

JUNE 6
PLAY WITH A YO-YO

Did you know that yo-yos have been around for thousands of years?

See how many times in a row you can throw and catch a yo-yo. Try some yo-yo tricks.

Keep practicing! It takes a while to get the hang of it. Then, try teaching a friend.

What other toys do you like to play with?

JUNE 7
DANCE LIKE A CRANE

Cranes are the tallest birds that can fly. These elegant animals are celebrated in June every year in Mongolia.

Cranes dance when they're excited, frustrated, or have lots of extra energy. They also dance when they want to show off.

Dance like a long-necked, long-legged crane today.

How do you feel when you dance?

JUNE 8
WORLD OCEANS DAY

On World Oceans Day, people around our blue planet
celebrate the ocean, which connects us all.

Oceans are home to spectacular plant and
animal life. They provide us with oxygen,
which we need to live and breathe.

Plan a trip to the ocean, an aquarium, or the library
to learn about life in these wondrous waters today.

What interests you about the ocean?

JUNE 9
SAY "OOPS!"

Spill your water?
Drop your cereal bowl?
Miss the goal?

When things don't go quite right today, just say "Oops!"
"Oops" is a silly word that's fun to say, and it means,
"I didn't mean to do that, but I can fix it!"

It's frustrating when things don't go the way we want.
Just remember, everyone makes mistakes.

JUNE 10
SHOW OFF YOUR STYLE

Whether you call them sunglasses, sunnies, or shades, these summer accessories are fantastic.

See without squinting.
Keep your eyes healthy.
Feel cool on hot summer days.
Show the world your style today.

JUNE 11
DRESS UP THE ORDINARY

In 2005, Magda Sayeg from Texas knitted a sleeve for her shop's door handle. People were delighted to discover a pop of cheer in an unexpected place. It inspired others all over the world to cover ordinary things with small "yarn bombs."

What ordinary object can you wrap with a blast of color today?

JUNE 12
DELIGHT IN
TINY TREATS

In the United States, they are called cupcakes.
In England, little cakes are known as fairy cakes.
In Australia, they are named patty cakes.

There's something so sweet about things
that come in small packages.

JUNE 13
TRY SEWING

Play around with putting materials
together in different ways today.
Ask a grown-up to help you.

You can use:
- Pieces of fabric,
felt, or old clothes
- Scissors
- A needle
- Thread
- Buttons

Don't worry if it's not perfect.
It's fun to try new things.

JUNE 14
DESIGN A FAMILY FLAG

In the United States, people celebrate Flag Day today. The U.S. flag has 50 stars to represent the 50 states.

Each state also has a flag. What does your state's flag look like? What do the colors or symbols mean?

Design a flag for your family today. What colors or symbols will you include? Fly your family flag with pride.

JUNE 15
ACTIVATE A SUPERPOWER

Did you know that we have a secret superpower?
It's the power to make ourselves feel good
and to make others around us feel good, too!
It's a smile.

It tells your brain you
feel happy and safe.

A smile is
a message.

Your muscles
relax and your
ability
to fight germs
gets a boost.

Others feel
welcome and
happy to see you.
Then they
smile, too!

JUNE 16
VISIT A FARMERS' MARKET

Farmers' markets are delicious places to explore.
Have fun wandering the stalls today.

Learn about the
flowers and plants
growing nearby.

Taste foods
made with local
ingredients.

Pick out new fruits
and vegetables
to try.

JUNE 17
DISCOVER TESSELLATIONS

Dutch artist M.C. Escher was born today in 1898. His artwork featured tessellation patterns of flat shapes with no gaps.

Tessellations can be found all around us: in art, clothing, floor tiles, and buildings. Look for interesting tessellations as you go through your day. Then, why not design a tessellation of your own?

JUNE 18
HAVE A PICNIC

Enjoy a meal outside today.

Pack a lunch . . .
Find a Spot . . .
Spread a blanket . . .
Breathe in fresh air . . .
Enjoy your food!

JUNE 19
SAY GOODBYE TO SPRING

The summer solstice is coming up.
Have a closing ceremony to mark the end of spring.

Go for a walk around your neighborhood
and take some time to think about the
things that you enjoyed this season.

What do you love about springtime?

Playing with my dog at the park!

JUNE 20
PLAY WITH BALANCE

Arms out wide like wings . . .
Heel to toe . . .
Heel to toe . . .
Can you walk the tightrope?

With our imagination, we can find
a little excitement anywhere.

JUNE 21
CELEBRATE MIDSUMMER

The summer solstice is the day with the longest period of
daylight. In the northern hemisphere, the summer solstice
is in late June and marks the beginning of summer.

People in Sweden call this time Midsummer and celebrate
by dancing around a maypole. Many weave flowers into
wreaths or crowns and embrace the idea that things
in nature have special powers.

How do you begin your summer?
What are you looking forward to this season?

JUNE 22
PLAY WITH BALLOONS

During a summer festival in Taiwan, people gather
to watch hundreds of hot-air balloons rise.
Giant orbs of color fill the open sky.

Today, play with keeping a balloon in the air
or take a walk holding a bunch of balloons.

Let yourself feel lifted up, just like the balloons.

JUNE 23
REACH FOR THE STARS

Engineers use math and science to design and
build new machines, buildings, and products.

Ellen Ochoa is an American astronaut who became the
first Hispanic woman to travel into space. She's also
invented several devices used in space exploration.

"Don't be afraid to reach for the stars," she says.

Setting and working towards a goal can be a big
source of joy. What is one of your goals?

JUNE 24
TRY UPCYCLING

Upcycling is turning something that would normally be thrown away into something that is useful, beautiful, or both!

Today, take notice of objects that you could transform, or change, to make into something else.

How great is it to do something that sparks your imagination and helps our Earth?

JUNE 25
MAKE A FRIENDSHIP NECKLACE

What do you like to do with friends?
Try making something together
today, like friendship necklaces.

It's nice to show how much we care about our friends.

JUNE 26
GIVE TO OTHERS

Do you have clothes, toys, or books that you don't need anymore and that others might enjoy? Consider donating things that are still in good shape to people who could really use them.

Your donations help other people and the environment, too.

JUNE 27
LEARN ABOUT
PINEAPPLE PLANTS

Apples grow on trees. Grapes grow on vines.
Pineapples grow on . . . plants! In fact, only one
pineapple at a time can grow on a plant.

Spiky on the outside, sweet on the inside, pineapples
are one of nature's treasures.

Think of as many fruits as you can.
Do you know how they grow?

JUNE 28
TAKE A CLOSER LOOK

Feed your curiosity today.
Use a magnifying glass, telescope, binoculars,
or even the zoom function on a mobile phone
to observe your environment in a new way.

What new and interesting details do you notice?

JUNE 29
BREAKFAST FOR DINNER

What do you eat for breakfast?
Waffles or pancakes?
Eggs and rice?
Cereal or porridge?

Try having your breakfast favorites for dinner today.

Sometimes doing things a little differently
makes a day feel even more special.

JUNE 30
WISH ON SHOOTING STARS

Rocks are everywhere . . . even in Space.
When rocks fall into Earth's atmosphere,
they make a hot streak through the air.
They appear as shooting stars in our night sky.

Shooting stars are good for making wishes.
What would you like to wish for today?

JULY 1
CELEBRATE THE HALF YEAR

Today is the first day of the second half of the year.
It's this year's half birthday!

Finding reasons to celebrate can make
any day more fun.

Figure out your half birthday.
Take the day you were born and add six months.
How would you like to celebrate it?

JULY 2
PLAY TENNIS

To play tennis, you need a racket, a ball, a net, and a friend.

It can be hard to hit a tennis ball and make it go where you want. You might miss the ball. You might not get it over the net, or you might send the ball off the court completely.

But when you actually hit the ball over the net, it feels great! And the more you play, the better you get.

Take a swing at tennis or another summer sport today.

JULY 3
KEEP COOL

July can be a very hot month. Give thanks today for all the things that keep you cool on hot, sticky days.

Sleeveless shirts

Shorts

Hats

Ice pops

Sunglasses

Fans

Shady trees

JULY 4
INDEPENDENCE DAY

In the United States, people celebrate Independence Day today. Families and friends gather to march in parades, eat red, white, and blue foods, and watch fireworks.

Fireworks are spectacular and awe-inspiring explosions of color and light in the dark sky.

Find ways to add sparkle and light to your day or night!

INVENT AN ICE CREAM FLAVOR

There are lots of interesting ice cream flavors. What's the wildest one you've seen or tasted?

Try combining different ingredients to invent your own ice cream flavor today. Experiment with a small scoop to start and see what you come up with. Is it yucky or yummy? Offer a sample taste to a friend. Do they like it?

Everyone has different tastes. That's a good thing.

JULY 6
PAINT LIKE FRIDA KAHLO

Frida Kahlo was born in Mexico on this day in 1907.
Frida was very sick when she was young. When she was
stuck in bed for a long time, she learned how to paint.

Through her paintings, she expressed her pain and
sadness as well as the things that made her happy,
such as animals and plants.

Try making a self-portrait. What could you draw
or paint that shows how you feel today?

Sometimes, we can feel both a little bit sad and a little
bit happy. Expressing how we feel can help us feel lighter.

JULY 7
MAKE MACARONI JEWELRY

Turn plain, dry pasta into jewelry, a costume piece,
a magical accessory, or a gift today.

You can use:
- Dry, uncooked pasta in any shape
- String
- Markers
- Paint
- Food coloring

Color your pasta, let it dry, then string it together.

Play around with different color combinations
or shades of the same color.

JULY 8
SPEND TIME IN A HAMMOCK

A hammock is a swinging bed or chair made of netting
or cloth. It's often stretched between two trees.
Reading, snuggling, or snoozing in a hammock is
a lovely way to spend a summer afternoon.

What special place
could you spend some
quiet time in today?

DECORATE ROCKS

Go on a rock hunt today and see what cool rocks
you uncover. Try decorating your rocks with markers,
paint, or chalk. Make a rock garden or fill a jar
of stones for a friend.

Spotting eye-catching natural things to collect
or share is something you can do anytime.

JULY 10
EAT FOOD ON A STICK

Have you ever eaten food on a stick?
Why not give it a try today?
Choose ingredients with different
flavors, shapes, and colors.

Breakfast on
a stick . . .

Sandwich
on a
stick . . .

Rainbow
on a stick . . .

Dessert
on a
stick!

NOTICE THE GREAT THINGS IN EVERY DAY LIKE E. B. WHITE

The children's book author E. B. White was born today in 1899. He wrote the book *Charlotte's Web*, a wonderful friendship story about a spider named Charlotte and a young pig named Wilbur.

E.B. got the idea for his book when he noticed a spiderweb in his barn. He was fascinated and delighted by animals.

Notice everyday things that you love today and write them down.

JULY 12
ENGAGE YOUR SENSES
AT THE BEACH

There are so many wonderful ways to
engage your senses at the beach.

Hear waves splash on the shore . . .
Feel sand in your toes . . .
See people swimming . . .
Smell the salty air . . .
Taste an ice cream!

What do you like to hear, feel, see, smell,
and taste at the beach?

EAT FRIED POTATOES

Fried potatoes have different names in different countries. You may know them as potato chips, French fries, or crisps.

You can eat them with ketchup, mayonnaise, cheese, spices, or even with gravy on top.

They can be long and skinny, thick, crinkled, or curly.

How do you like to eat fried potatoes?

JULY 14
ENJOY SUMMER YOGA

Today, find some space outdoors.
Move through these sunny yoga poses.

Surf the waves

Shine like the sun

Scuttle like a crab

JULY 15
TASTE SUMMER FRUITS

Summer is a delicious time when sweet, juicy fruits are in season. Enjoy some of these fresh fruits today. When you eat them outdoors, they can taste even better.

Papayas

Plums

Lychees

Cherries

Watermelon

Peaches

JULY 16
ADORE CUTE CREATURES

With their fluffy bodies, long whiskers, big eyes,
and tiny ears, guinea pigs are so cute!

These little creatures are gentle, friendly, and when
they're happy, they jump up in the air like popping popcorn.

What are three animals that you think are cute?
Look at some pictures or videos of them today.
Or, if you have an animal at home, give it
a loving squeeze.

JULY 17
SEND EMOJIS

"Emoji" is an expression that originates from Japan and roughly means "picture word."

Emojis are one of many ways we can communicate and express ourselves. And they're very cute and fun!

Explore emojis today.

Choose your favorites.

Send a fun message to a friend.

JULY 18
SPEND 67 MINUTES FOR GOOD

Nelson Mandela was a civil-rights activist and the president of South Africa. He was born on this date in 1918. Mandela believed in equality, peace, and freedom for all South Africans regardless of their race and skin color.

On his birthday, people around the world are encouraged to spend 67 minutes helping others. This is to honor the 67 years that Mandela spent dedicating his life to the people of South Africa.

Spend part of your day lending a helping hand today.

If everyone dedicates a little bit of time, we can make the world a more peaceful and joyful place.

JULY 19
PLAY CHESS

Chess is a game invented in India around 1,500 years ago.

To play, you need two players, a chess board, and a set of pieces that include a king, queen, knights, and rooks (or castles). Each type of piece can move in a different way.

Both kids and adults enjoy playing chess. Players plan how to move a piece and think about what could happen next. The game takes strategy and practice.

Games that challenge our minds can give
joy and satisfaction.

JULY 20
OBSERVE THE MOON

Look up at the moon tonight and every night this week.

Draw how the sky and moon look each night.

The moon appears to be a different shape depending on the positions of the moon, the Earth, and the Sun. Seeing the moon wax (get bigger) or wane (get smaller) reminds us of the connection between these incredible bodies in space.

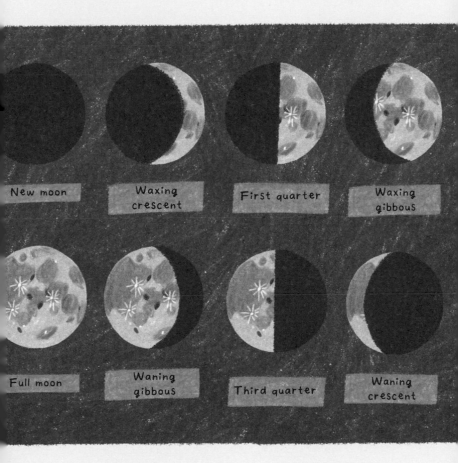

New moon

Waxing crescent

First quarter

Waxing gibbous

Full moon

Waning gibbous

Third quarter

Waning crescent

What do you like about the moon?

JULY 21
PICK SUMMER FLOWERS

Summer is a gorgeous season.
Keep an eye out for these blooming flowers.

Allium

Black-Eyed Susans

Echinacea

Geraniums

What flowers would you pick to put in a vase on
your kitchen table or to grow in a garden?

JULY 22
EAT MANGOES

Mangoes are the national fruit of the Philippines, Pakistan, and India. In fact, in India, if you want to give a thoughtful gift to a friend, you give a basket of mangoes!

Taste some of this delicious fruit today. You can slice up a fresh one or throw some frozen pieces in a blender to make a cool drink.

What makes this sweet treat even better? When you share it with a friend!

JULY 23
TOSS WATER BALLOONS

Have a bit of fun today by taking turns tossing a balloon
filled with water back and forth with a friend.

Start facing each other and stand a few feet apart.
One person tosses the balloon and the other tries
to catch it without it popping.
If the balloon doesn't burst open, both friends
take a big step backward.
Toss the balloon again.
Keep tossing and taking a step back . . .
until the balloon pops! Splash!

JULY 24
CELEBRATE COUSINS

Gatherings with cousins are filled with . . .

Giggles

Love

Jokes

Silliness

Games

Races

Today, call a cousin or someone special in your family
and make a plan for what you'd like to do together.

JULY 25
GO ON A RIDE

Have you ever been to a theme park or to the funfair?

Do you enjoy rides that . . .

Go fast . . .   Spin in a circle . . .

Bump and crash . . .   Or take in the view?

Some people like the funny feeling in their tummies when
they go on rides. Some people don't. Either is just fine.
There's something fun for everyone.

JULY 26
TAKE A WALK BY THE PIER

Have you ever walked by the water on a pier?
Some are quiet, and others are bustling with
arcade games and places to eat.

Take a walk by the water if you can today.
Look for things that interest you out on
the water and where you are on land.

JULY 27
SING SILLY SONGS

Singing a silly song is a great way to entertain yourself or to entertain your family. You can make your song rhyme . . . or not!
What silly words do you like to say or sing?

Sing them LOUD . . .

Sing them soft . . .

Sing them in an opera voice . . .

Sing them while you get up and shake your body!

Make up a silly song and try to get it stuck in someone else's head today. When they start singing it, you'll feel so pleased.

JULY 28
SEND A HUG

Sometimes we want to give someone a hug
but they're too far away. Send a hug instead!

Draw a picture of yourself with your arms outstretched.
Color yourself in.
Write a message.
Fold up your "hug," pop it in a big envelope,
and send your surprise.

We can find lots of creative ways to send love.

JULY 29
SPREAD RAINBOW CHEER

Summer showers can make magnificent rainbows.

Look up. Is there a rainbow? Call out, "There's a rainbow!"
You don't want anyone to miss it.

If you don't see one today, why not make a rainbow on
the pavement with chalk for someone to stumble upon?

You can make someone smile from unexpected
colorful joy.

SET UP A LEMONADE STAND

Who's thirsty on a hot Summer day? Everyone!

Set up a lemonade Stand in your neighborhood today.

You can offer your neighbors a cool, refreshing drink.
What a joyful way to Spend an afternoon.

JULY 31
MARVEL AT FIREFLIES

It's a delight to see the flicker of fireflies
on a summer evening.

Fireflies, also known as lightning bugs, communicate with
each other through light-flashing patterns. Each species
has its own unique pattern.

Look for these glowing creatures tonight, hovering in the
night air. Try catching them in a jar or by cupping your
hands. See them flicker, then set them free again!

AUGUST 1
CREATE YOUR OWN OLYMPICS

The modern summer Olympics are held every four years.
The idea of the Olympic Games originated in ancient
Greece almost 3,000 years ago.

Olympic athletes are so inspiring. They are strong,
dedicated, and work on getting better every day.
Isn't it amazing what the human body can do?

Create your own Olympic events today.
Compete with yourself to beat your best time
or play against some friends.
See what amazing things your body can do!

AUGUST 2
MAKE YOUR SISTER SMILE

Do you have a sister or someone who is like a sister to you? Today is a great day to let them know how much they mean to you.

What do you like to do together?
What makes your sister laugh?
How does your sister make you laugh?

Give your sister a hug today and
see if you can make each other smile.

AUGUST 3
DO THINGS BACK TO FRONT

Shake things up today by doing things back to front.

Wear socks on your head and hats on your feet.
Greet your friends with, "Morning good! You are how?"
For dinner, eat dessert first and enjoy the taste.
Then, snuggle into bed and rest your feet on your pillow.
Tomorrow morning, the world will look different!

AUGUST 4
COLOR

Take a few minutes to sit at the table and color today.
Maybe you can listen to some music at the same time.

There's something soothing and peaceful about coloring.

When you're done with your picture, you can hang it up
or give it to someone. If you're not finished, then
put it away to finish another day.

AUGUST 5
MOVE IN THE SUN

Summer is fantastic for all the different ways you can move your body.

What are your favorite ways to move outside in summer?

Hiking

Dribbling

Scoring

Skipping

Riding

CELEBRATE TOMATOES

Tomatoes are some of the most popular fruits to grow in gardens, and they taste extra delicious in the summertime.

Celebrate these juicy cheerful fruits today and all the yummy ways to eat them.

How do you like to eat tomatoes?

Pasta sauce

Tomato bruschetta

Plain

Tomato kachumber

Tomato soup

AUGUST 7
LIGHT YOUR WAY

Experiment with a flashlight this evening.

Explore under your bed.
Create shadow puppets.
Make the light dance on your ceiling.

Find entertainment by looking at your
surroundings in a different way.

AUGUST 8
ROLL DOWN A HILL

Sometimes all you need is a grassy hill on
a hot summer's day to have the best time.

Find a clear path.
Lay down.
Launch!
Say, "Wheeeee!"

When do you like going
fast or feeling dizzy?

AUGUST 9
INTERNATIONAL DAY OF THE WORLD'S INDIGENOUS PEOPLES

Indigenous people are the earliest people to live in a place. There are millions of indigenous people around the world, and this day raises awareness of the challenges faced by indigenous communities.

The Māori are the indigenous people of New Zealand and greet each other by saying, "kia ora" (key-a-or-ah). This translates to "have life" or "be healthy." They use this phrase to say "hello." Practice saying, "kia ora" today!

kia ora!

Connecting with people and learning about their culture is a great way to feel happiness and joy.

AUGUST 10
FLY A KITE

In Bali, an island in Indonesia, August is a very windy month. People celebrate by hosting a big kite festival with competitions such as most unusual design or longest flight. As the kites with their long flowing ribbon tails take off, an orchestra plays music, filling the spectators with joyful excitement.

What kind of kite would you like to fly?

What could you do to turn a breezy day into an exciting day?

PLAY IN THE SAND

Scoop it.
Spread it.
Pack it.
Pile it.
Draw in it.
Dig in it.
Play in it.

Sand has a unique texture.
What do you like to feel in your hands?

AUGUST 12
WORLD ELEPHANT DAY

There are so many reasons to love elephants.

Elephants are wonderful animals that naturally live in Africa and Asia. They are the largest land animals, very gentle and extremely smart.

These stunning creatures have great memories and big emotions. They can cry when something upsets them, and they can make loud trumpeting sounds when they feel happy. They love to swim and play in water . . . and they love bananas!

Learn more about elephants today and tell others about them. When we appreciate wild animals, we work harder to protect them.

AUGUST 13
PLAY WITH LETTERS AND WORDS

Calligraphy is the art of beautiful handwriting.

Look for calligraphy on T-shirts, posters, invitations, or signs. Then play with writing letters or words in a way that makes you feel happy today.

AUGUST 14
GO FOR A SWING

Swoop up.
Swoosh back.
Legs pump.
Legs tuck.

Keep soaring
higher and higher.
Keep smiling
wider and wider.

How do you feel when you're on a swing?

AUGUST 15
SEARCH FOR YELLOW

Yellow is such a cheerful, sunny color.
Go on a scavenger hunt and
search for yellow things today.

Bumblebee yellow

Mustard yellow

Buttery yellow

Lemon yellow

Golden yellow

Bright yellow

Dandelion yellow

AUGUST 16
GO FOR A SWIM

Going swimming is so fun.
How do you like to move in the water?

Float on your back

Dive deep

Stand on
your hands

Play ball

Jump wildly

AUGUST 17
HAVE AN OUTDOOR MOVIE NIGHT

With nice summer weather, you can do lots of entertaining things outside, including watching movies!

See if there are any local places hosting outdoor movie screenings, on rooftops, in parks, or at drive-in theaters.

Bring a blanket, a comfy chair, and a bowl of popcorn to enjoy a movie night under the stars.

AUGUST 18
REVEL IN COLORS

In the city of St John's in Newfoundland, Canada, there's a neighborhood of brightly painted houses known as Jellybean Row. These sweet-colored homes stand out even on misty, rainy days. What would a town painted like your favorite sweets look like?

When you're in places where you feel happy, pay attention to the colors that surround you. Maybe they're beachy blues on a sunny day at the ocean, grassy greens and browns when you're playing in a park, or the light pastels of all the flavors in an ice cream shop.

AUGUST 19
EXPLORE IMAGINARY WORLDS

What imaginary worlds bring you happiness?
Are they from a book, a video game, or a television show?
Or are they worlds you make up yourself with your toys?

Enjoy spending time using your imagination today.

DIG FOR WORMS

Go exploring after a warm summer rainstorm.
Earthworms need to stay moist, so they're easy to
find when the ground is a bit wet.

Can you find any worms crawling up to the surface?
Move as quietly as possible so your vibrations don't
scare them away.

Look under rocks, logs, or piles of leaves.
Watch them dig and burrow.

Worms help nourish soil so plants can grow.
It's great to see nature up close.

AUGUST 21
MEMORIZE A POEM

What kinds of poems do you enjoy? Silly ones?
Poems that tell a story? Poems that rhyme?

Find a poem you like and try memorizing it.
It's a fun challenge for your memory, and it can
make you feel proud. There's joy in saying the
words and feeling the rhythm of each line.

When you know a poem by heart, recite it for other
people. Hearing a poem can make others happy!
And it might inspire them to memorize one, too.

AUGUST 22
FIND A BARGAIN

Have you ever been to a garage sale?

It can be a delight to sift through strange
collections of items. You might discover something
that sparks joy for you, and it might feel extra
special to get it at a bargain.

What are some of your favorite items?
Do you remember where you got them?

AUGUST 23
TAKE A TWILIGHT WALK

Twilight is a time between day and night, when the sun has gone down but there's still light in the sky. Sometimes the atmosphere can fill with beautiful shades of pinks and purples.

Go for a walking adventure at twilight, and see what the sky looks like where you live.
What colors do you see? What sounds do you hear?
Take a deep breath in. What do you smell?

AUGUST 24
ADD SPRINKLES

In Australia, people spread butter on bread and top it
with sprinkles to make a treat called 'fairy bread'.

A scattering of lots of colors can make simple
things feel fun.

Try adding sprinkles to the food you eat today.

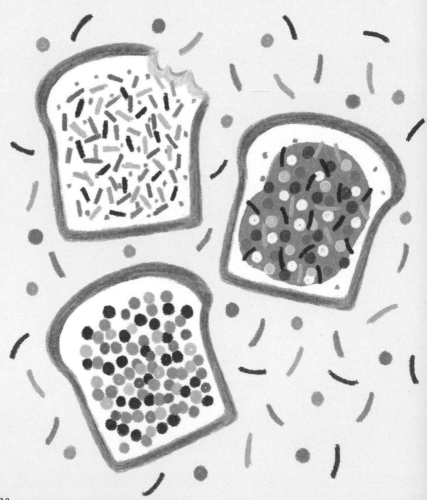

AUGUST 25
TAKE A MENTAL PICTURE

When you find yourself having a happy moment today, pause for a few seconds and take a mental picture: a photo using just your mind.

Look at what's around you, close your eyes, and picture the image in your head. Take a slow, deep breath in, let it out and say, "click."

At the end of your day, flip through your collection of mental pictures. You can experience double the fun when you recall the moments that make you smile.

AUGUST 26
CHERISH FURRY FRIENDS

Give three cheers for loyal, furry, fun-loving dogs!

Whether they're small enough to fit in the palm of your hand or almost as big as a bear, dogs light up when they see us, and we light up in return.

If you have a playful pup, give it some extra care today. If you don't, look for some dogs out for a walk. Give a wave and say, "hello!" If you see its tail wag, you just made that dog's day.

AUGUST 27
GO BANANAS

A bunch of bananas is a familiar everyday sight.
Have you ever thought about how wonderful bananas are?

They're easy to bring along. Just grab and go!

They're fantastic in recipes.

They contain vitamins and minerals that keep us healthy.

They're the silliest fruit and can really make us smile.

AUGUST 28
STYLE WITH WASHI TAPE

Have you ever experimented with different kinds
of tape? What kinds do you like? How do you use them?

Play with beautiful Japanese-inspired washi tapes today.

Add a cute border
to a plain plant pot.

Make a photo book
to send to a friend.

Use layered tape to make
memorable gift tags.

Make everyday things more joyful with craft supplies.

AUGUST 29
SPOT SMILING FACES

Play an observation game and look for happy things
as you move through your day.

See if you spot anything that looks like a smiling face.

Point out what you find and ask others if they
can see it, too.

Can you mimic the faces you find?

AUGUST 30
FEEL CONTENT AT BEDTIME

Enjoy the routine of getting ready for bed
tonight by checking in with your senses.

Taste toothpaste
in a fresh and
clean mouth.

Feel soft
pajamas and a
comfortable bed.

Smell soap from
your shower
or bath.

See the pages
of a friendly
bedtime story.

Hear, "Sleep
well, I love you!"

Say, "Goodnight,
I love you!"

What parts of bedtime make you feel especially
calm, relaxed, and loved?

CELEBRATE RITUALS

Ganesh Chaturthi is a ten-day Hindu festival celebrated around this time of year to honor Ganesha, the god of prosperity and wisdom.

At the start of the festival, idols of Ganesha are placed in homes and offered coconut, flowers, and 21 modaks (sweet dumplings).

For Hindu people, ceremonies for Ganesha bring good luck.

What rituals do you know to bring good luck?

SEPTEMBER 1
GET READY FOR SCHOOL

September marks the return to school in many places.

It's time to
find your school
supplies!

You might shop for a
few new things, too.

Give them a fresh look
for the new term.

What school supplies make you excited for the new year?

SEPTEMBER 2
SIGN UP FOR A LIBRARY CARD

Do you have a library card?
If not, September is a good time to get one.

There's no place like the library.

Where else can you take out anything that you
like for free and return it when you're done?

It's wonderful that everyone in the community
can get together to share books.

SEPTEMBER 3
WATCH THE CLOUDS

Lay back and look up at the sky today.
What do the clouds look like to you?

Try taking a Big Cloud Breath.
Breathe in as you imagine floating on a fluffy cloud.
Breathe out like you are blowing a cloud away.

SEPTEMBER 4
DISCOVER NATURE FORTS

Take a walk and be on the lookout for nature forts: secret hideaways where you can crawl in and make a magical and enchanting place.

What natural objects will you transform? Will you slay dragons, mix magic potions, prepare for a quest, or cook up a delicious dish?

SEPTEMBER 5
TINKER AROUND

Tinker trays are great places to keep
little odds and ends to reuse.

Take things apart.
Investigate them.
Combine parts.
Think some more.
Try again.
Create something new.

What do you like to tinker with?

SEPTEMBER 6
MAKE YOUR BED

Making your bed in the morning is a quick way
to start off a great day.

Smooth out your sheets, pull up your blankets, fluff
up your pillow, and settle your stuffed animals.

You'll see your small accomplishment right away and
have more space to play. Your room will look tidier
and that will help you feel calm and confident.

And at the end of a long day, getting into
a clear and comfy space feels good.

SEPTEMBER 7
HANG UP HAPPY REMINDERS

Take a look at your room and your bedroom door.
Is there anything you want to change or update?
Maybe you have a photograph from the summer, a new
piece of artwork, a postcard from a trip, or a certificate
you want to display to remind you of a happy moment.

Find a spot and hang it up. How does it look?

If your room feels great the way it is, that's fantastic!
Smile and soak it in.

SEPTEMBER 8
SAY SORRY

Sometimes we hurt others on purpose or by accident, and we feel bad. Saying, "I'm sorry," can help the other person feel better and can help us feel better, too.

We can face hard moments with kindness.

SEPTEMBER 9
TAKE CARE OF YOUR TEDDY

Do you have a teddy that brings you comfort?
Maybe you like to hold it when you cuddle up
to read a book, watch a movie or go to sleep.

Give your teddy some extra love and care today.
You could put it in the wash, brush its fur, tidy the
area around it, and give it an extra-long squeeze.

It feels good to take care of things that
help us feel happy.

SEPTEMBER 10
CELEBRATE THE MOON

Mid-Autumn Festival, also known as Moon Festival or Harvest Moon Festival, is observed mainly in Chinese and Vietnamese communities during the full moon in September or early October, depending on the lunar calendar. Its tradition is based on celebrating the sun in the spring and the moon in the autumn.

People gather with their families for dinner then drink tea and eat delicious mooncakes, small pastries with a thin crust and a filling in the middle such as sweet red bean paste.

For what special occasions do you eat cakes?

SEPTEMBER 11
LOOK FOR LIGHT

Tribute in Light is the name of an annual art project that commemorates the fall of the Twin Towers on September 11, 2001 in New York. Eighty-eight powerful light bulbs combine together to shine four miles into the sky to resemble the shape of the two skyscrapers.

Tributes can be anything meant to share and help keep memories of something special alive.
They can provide comfort and peace.

SEPTEMBER 12
POSE FOR A PICTURE

Who adores photos of kids? Grandparents!
Pose for a fun family picture today.
Send it to your grandparents or other
people in your family along with a note.

A photo of a happy you is a treasured gift.

What could you say in your message that
would be sure to make them smile?

SEPTEMBER 13
WATCH SEASONS CHANGE

Autumn is coming soon. It's a season known for the leaves changing from shades of green into spectrums of red, yellow, orange, and brown. Start paying attention to the trees.

Take a picture or make a sketch of a tree in your neighborhood each week starting now and continuing through autumn. At the end of the season, you can even make a flipbook with your pictures.

Watching how nature changes over time can be quietly spectacular.

SEPTEMBER 14
LEARN ABOUT RED PANDAS

Have you ever heard of red pandas?

Despite their name, they're not related to black-and-white pandas. Red pandas are much smaller and about the size of a cat. They live in the Himalaya Mountains and are sometimes called the Himalayan raccoon, a bear cat, or firefox.

What would you name the red panda? It can be a fun game to rename things based on other things they resemble.

Give it a try today.

SEPTEMBER 15
HISPANIC HERITAGE MONTH

Today is the start of Hispanic Heritage Month in the
United States. It recognizes the contributions and
achievements made by Hispanic Americans. On this date,
the Latin American countries Costa Rica, El Salvador,
Guatemala, Honduras, and Nicaragua celebrate their
independence. Mexico and Chile's independence days
follow later in the month.

Festivities include parades, dancing, and music. Latin
music has strong rhythms that make you want to move!

Claves

Pandeiro

Congas

Maracas

There are many different types of Latin music.
Listen to some today and see how it makes you feel.

SEPTEMBER 16
PAINT WITH WATERCOLORS

Watercolor paints are so much fun to play around with.

Experiment with different sized brushes.
Try a mini canvas or a giant one.
Use a lot of color or just a little.

Mix . . .   Spread . . .   Swirl . . .

Blend . . .   Stroke . . .   Splatter!

Notice how you feel while you're moving the brush
across the surface. Then, proudly show off your
paintings when they're dry.

SEPTEMBER 17
HOPSCOTCH AND HULA HOOP

Do you have a bit of chalk and a little space?

Make a hopscotch board or an obstacle course.

Have a hoop? See how long you can keep it swinging. How long can you keep it rolling?

What other games could you invent today?

SEPTEMBER 18
ENJOY RIVERS

Rivers are important waterways for our planet,
and they're terrific for exploring.

Clean up.

Race sticks.

Watch bugs.

Skip stones.

Nature has such fantastic playgrounds.

SEPTEMBER 19
TALK LIKE A PIRATE

Ahoy, mateys! Encourage your friends to talk like a pirate today. Grab your eye patch and say, "Arrrr!"

SEPTEMBER 20
HOST AN OUTDOOR PARTY

Host an outdoor party with friends while the weather is still warm. Invite everyone to bring food to share.

Maybe you can even challenge everyone to bring something made with the same ingredient, such as strawberries!

Strawberry juice

Strawberry cake

Strawberries dipped in chocolate

Strawberry sweets

Strawberry ice pops

SEPTEMBER 21
DANCE AROUND

An American band called Earth, Wind & Fire have a song about dancing on the twenty-first night of September.

Give it a listen today. Dance around your living room or outside in the fresh air and chase the clouds away.

Tomorrow you can ask, "Do you remember the twenty-first night of September?" and dance all over again!

SEPTEMBER 22
NOTICE NUMBERS

Numbers play a big part in all our lives.

Today, notice all the different ways numbers are used.
They do so much to help organize our world.
Can you think of three ways we use numbers
in things that make you happy?

Dates

Sports

Money

Measurements

Maps

SEPTEMBER 23
INTERNATIONAL DAY OF SIGN LANGUAGE

Did you know that there are more than 70 million deaf people in the world and 300 different sign languages?

This day raises awareness of the importance of sign language and the human rights of people who are deaf.

Understanding and connecting with others is one of the best ways we can find friendship and joy.

SEPTEMBER 24
FLY HELICOPTER SEEDS

Different kinds of trees make different kinds of seeds.

Some trees, like maple, ash, elm, and sycamore, make
samaras or "helicopter seeds." These winged seeds are
also known as whirlybirds or twisters. Can you guess why?
They can twirl when they fall from tree branches or
when you launch them! They float away from the
wide-reaching branches of their parent tree
and grow where there's more sunlight.

Look for helicopter seeds today and throughout autumn.
Toss them high into the air and enjoy watching them spin.

SEPTEMBER 25
WISH FOR SWEETNESS AND HEALTH

Rosh Hashanah is the celebration of the Jewish new year, taking place in September. It's the beginning of a ten-day period of holidays ending with Yom Kippur, the holiest day in the Jewish calendar.

People celebrate Rosh Hashanah by dipping apples in honey to symbolize a sweet and healthy new year.

If you were to create a food tradition, what would it be?

SEPTEMBER 26
WEAR A HOODED SWEATSHIRT

In autumn, a day can go from warm to chilly from one moment to the next. A hooded sweatshirt helps us feel just right, not too hot and not too cold.

Wear one today and take a moment to appreciate the comfort it brings.

Lots of colors and styles.

An attached hood in case your ears get cold.

A zipper for making it easy to put on and take off.

Big pockets for keeping important things and for keeping hands warm.

SEPTEMBER 27
WATCH SQUIRRELS

Squirrels are hard at work in September when many trees begin dropping seeds. These nimble animals bury thousands of nuts, seeds, and acorns to prepare their food supply for the cold winter.

See what you can learn about squirrels by taking a closer look today. Observe how they collect, scamper, and hide their food. Watch how they wrinkle their noses and nibble their snacks.

Why do you think they flick their fluffy tails?

It's fascinating what you see when you slow down to look.

SEPTEMBER 28
SHOW OFF YOUR TALENTS

Can you sing the alphabet back to front?
Twist like a pretzel?
Bend over backward?
Roll your tongue?
Snap your fingers?
Wiggle your ears?

Show off one of your unique talents
today, or try to learn a new one!

Feeling
proud is
joyful.

SEPTEMBER 29
SURPRISE A NEIGHBOR

Planning small surprises can add a little excitement to your day. What could you do for a neighbor that would startle them in a happy way today?

Maybe you could make them a wildflower bouquet, a jar of treats, or leave a cheerful painting outside their door.

What kind of face do you think they'll make when they find it?

A little Surprise for you!

Do you like surprises?

SEPTEMBER 30
HAVE A WARM DRINK

A warm drink is so comforting on cool autumn days.

Sip a cup of hot mulled apple juice today.
Take in how it smells, tastes, and feels.
Mmm . . . the apple juice, cinnamon sticks,
orange peel, and spices.

What scents remind you of autumn?

OCTOBER 1
GO ON AN AUTUMN WALK

Go for a walk today and take in what's
happening in nature.

Listen to crunching leaves.
See shades of gold, orange, and red.
Feel snapping sticks under your feet.
What do you smell on your walk?
When you get home, taste something
warm and yummy.

OCTOBER 2
ENJOY AUTUMN YOGA

Autumn features big changes in nature.
Changes can be beautiful, exciting, and hard work.

Today, move through these autumn yoga poses.

Bird flying south

Changing leaves

Chipmunk
collecting acorns

OCTOBER 3
LOOK UP

Take a ride outside today on your scooter, on your bike,
or maybe in a wagon pulled by a tractor . . . and look up.

What can you see?
Are the trees' leaves dancing in the wind?
Are there butterflies fluttering above?
Listen for squirrels who may be
making their home.

OCTOBER 4
PICK APPLES

One of the great things about autumn is apple picking and tasting a juicy apple right off the tree.

Climb.
Pick.
Crunch.
Smile.

Take a bite of an apple today.
How would you describe the flavor?

OCTOBER 5
WORLD TEACHERS' DAY

On this day every year, teachers are celebrated worldwide. Teachers are fantastic people in our lives. Think of a time a teacher has helped you.

Learn more about your teacher today by asking:
What do you like to do on the weekend?
What is your favorite color?
What is your favorite animal?
Do you have any siblings?

What can you do to help your teacher feel appreciated?

OCTOBER 6
MAKE POPCORN

Pop, pop, pop!

You can pop it on the stove or make it in the microwave.
Either way, a bowl of popcorn is a simple delight.

Do you like popcorn plain, with butter, or sweet and salty?

Who could you eat popcorn with today?

OCTOBER 7
ENJOY MUSIC LIKE YO-YO MA

Yo-Yo Ma is a Chinese American musician. He was born in Paris, France, on this day in 1955. Yo-Yo Ma learned to play the cello when he was only four years old and is now one of the most famous cellists of all time.

Yo-Yo Ma believes that music is a wonderful way to connect with others and to express big feelings like joy and happiness.

Listen to Yo-Yo Ma's music today.
What musical instrument would you enjoy playing?

OCTOBER 8
KICK A BALL AROUND

Kick a ball around with some friends today.

Dribble . . .
Pass . . .
Shoot . . .
Score!

How do you like to play outside in October?

OCTOBER 9
ADMIRE THE ALPHABET

Hangul Day is celebrated in South Korea on this day. It's a national holiday that honors the invention of the Korean alphabet in 1446.

Being able to read and write stories, messages, thoughts and ideas brings us so much joy.

Take time today to admire the Korean alphabet today. Can you write the word "hi" in Korean?

안녕하세요
Hi
(ann-yeong-ha-se-yo)

친구
Friend
(chin-gu)

사랑해요
I love you
(sa-rang-hae-yo)

미안해요
Sorry
(mi-an-hae-yo)

가족
Family
(ga-jok)

OCTOBER 10
HAVE A SACK RACE

Gather some old sacks or big pillowcases.
Set up a course with start and finish lines.
Then, hop to it!

How fast and how far can you hop before
falling down in a fit of giggles?

OCTOBER 11
SPRINKLE KINDNESS

Surprise a stranger with an act of kindness today
and sprinkle a little joy into their day.

You could leave a happy note in a library book
for the next reader to discover.

Maybe your small act of kindness will inspire others
to sprinkle joy into someone else's day.

What other ideas can you come up with?

OCTOBER 12
PLAY "WOULD YOU RATHER?"

While waiting in line or eating dinner today,
play a question game to pass the time.

Take turns asking each other questions.
Would you rather . . .

. . . turn into a
dolphin
or a falcon?

. . . swim in a pool
filled with puppies
or spaghetti?

. . . be invisible
or superstrong?

. . . live in
space or
underwater?

. . . shrink down to
the size of an ant
or grow as large
as a dinosaur?

. . . control
water or the
wind?

Have fun comparing your answers and
explaining your choices.

OCTOBER 13
PICK PUMPKINS

Pumpkins can be so joyful!

They come in a variety of sizes and shapes.
They can be smooth, bumpy, or striped.
And they come in all different colors.

What kinds of pumpkins make you happy?

OCTOBER 14
DECORATE FOR AUTUMN

It's nice to decorate for the autumn season.
What kinds of decorations make you feel cheerful?

Wreaths

Pumpkins

Haystacks

Blooms

What autumnal decorations do you see where you live?

OCTOBER 15
REPAIR BROKEN ITEMS

Fixing things that are broken is a fantastic way to save money. It also helps the Earth by creating less waste.

You can repair with:

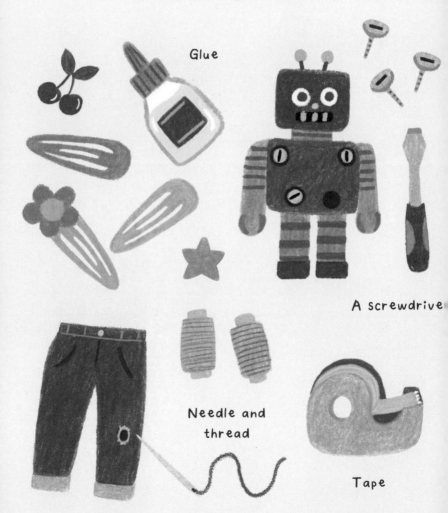

Glue

A screwdrive

Needle and thread

Tape

Repairing things can make you feel proud. What is something you could repair yourself?

OCTOBER 16
WORLD FOOD DAY

Today people around the world appreciate the amazing food that we have the privilege of eating. But World Food Day is also about raising awareness for people who do not have such privilege. Many families struggle to have enough to eat.

Take time to notice the food in your fridge and cupboards. Before every meal, pause to be thankful for the food on your plate.

What food in your fridge and cupboards can you donate? You can help! And helping feels great.

START A LEAF COLLECTION

Get outside and touch what's happening in nature.

Pick up leaves that are especially interesting or unique and start a collection today.

Look closely at the leaves you find. See if you can identify the different types of trees by their leaves.

Maple

Beech

Oak

Ginkgo

Horse chestnut

What kinds of trees grow where you live?

OCTOBER 18
MAKE A LEAF RUBBING

Take advantage of the bright colors in nature to make
your own spectacular art.

Put a leaf upside down on a table.
Place a piece of thin, light-colored paper over the leaf.
Rub across the paper using the side of a crayon.

You can use one color or a combination.
You can feature one leaf or many.

Making art from natural objects feels special.

OCTOBER 19
MAKE A READING NOOK

Create a reading nook today.

A seat, a pillow, a blanket,
a pile of books, and you!

What books have you been reading recently?

OCTOBER 20
SMILE AT SLOTHS

Sloths are known as slow and sleepy animals.
But there's so much more to these cute creatures
from Central and South America.

Sloths have long claws that make it hard for them to
stand on the ground. That's part of why they're so slow.
But their claws also help them hang upside down from
trees using no effort at all. They can't walk well,
but they are excellent swimmers and
can hold their breath for 40
minutes underwater!

What feature of sloths do you think is the most
interesting? Do you have anything in common with sloths?

OCTOBER 21
EAT DATES

Different fruits and vegetables are in season around the globe. In Morocco, dates are harvested in October.

Dates contain lots of vitamins and minerals that help our muscles. They can be eaten fresh off trees, or dried and eaten whenever.

Dates are especially important for Muslims. They're a common snack during religious holidays. Sometimes, when people have visitors to their homes, they offer their guests dates and a glass of milk to help them feel welcome.

How can you help someone feel welcome?

OCTOBER 22
MAKE A DIFFERENCE

Make a Difference Day takes place at the end of
October every year. It is all about making a difference,
large or small. People are encouraged to help others and
to make the world safer and fairer for all.

When a group of people is treated unfairly, we can:

Speak out   Work together

Listen   Stand up

We can do things to help our neighborhood,
community, and planet, today and every day.
Our actions make a difference.

OCTOBER 23
CARVE PUMPKINS

The tradition of carving pumpkins comes from Ireland.

In an old story, a ghost of a man named Jack wandered around in the night with only a lantern made from a piece of lighted coal in a carved-out turnip. To scare away Jack and other ghosts, people began to make their own lanterns by carving scary faces into pumpkins or turnips and putting them in windows or near doors.

Do you enjoy spooky stories? Would you like to carve a spooky pumpkin or a silly one?

MAKE A COSTUME

Making costumes is a blast, so try it today.

You can add a pair of glasses and become
a character from your favorite book.

You can put together what you already have
and transform into a favorite animal or superhero.

You can imagine, design, build, and embellish
to invent someone completely new.

What kinds of costumes make you feel confident?

OCTOBER 25
PLAY IN LEAVES

Make a giant mountain of leaves today.

Rake

Pile

Leap

Toss

Repeat!

OCTOBER 26
NAME THE FULL MOON

Some Native American people have traditional names for the full moon in every month. Each tribe's October moon name reflects things happening in nature.

Potawatomi:
First frost

Cree:
Birds fly south

Haida:
Bears
hibernate

Cherokee:
Harvest moon

Abenaki:
Leaf falling

What would you name October's full moon?

OCTOBER 27
APPRECIATE BLACK CATS

Black cats seem mysterious and magical, don't they?

With striking eyes and fur as dark as night, you can find them on lots of Halloween decor in October.

You can find real ones at animal shelters. Black cats don't get adopted as quickly. But black cats are purr-fect pets, and anyone would be lucky to have them.

If you're thinking of getting a new pet, check out your local adoption shelters to find a happy match for your home.

OCTOBER 28
GET LOST IN A CORN MAZE

Corn mazes are a fun autumn activity.

They're made by cutting different
paths into a big cornfield.

Getting lost in a maze can be fun,
with all the twists and turns.

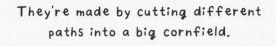

Finding your way
out is joyful, too!

OCTOBER 29
FIND JOY IN A RAINY DAY

Some people think of rainy days as grey and gloomy.
But there are plenty of cheerful colors, patterns,
and textures on rainy days if you look out for them.

Spot a rainbow, step in a puddle, search for worms.

What makes you happy when rain falls?

Rainbows

Umbrellas

Rain boots

Raindrops streaming
down windows

Worms . . . they
love the rain!

OCTOBER 30
PLAY CATCH

Toss . . .
Catch!
Miss?
Try again!

How many times in a row can you go without dropping
the ball? Keep trying to break your record.

OCTOBER 31
HALLOWEEN

There are so many things to be excited about on Halloween!

HALLOWEEN

Spooky decorations

Parties

Sweets

Costumes

Games

Trick-or-treating

What makes you happy on Halloween?

NOVEMBER 1
GROW GRATITUDE

November is a terrific month for growing gratitude. Gratitude is paying attention to the good things in our lives and being thankful for what we have.

Create a jar of gratitude seeds today.

1. Gather a big jar, ribbon, colorful strips of paper, and pens.

2. Decorate your jar.

Card from Grandma ♥

Jumping in leaves

3. Each day in November, write down one thing you're grateful for.

4. Feel your gratitude seeds grow into happy feelings.

NOVEMBER 2
SHARE MEMORIES

In Mexico, today is known as Día de los Muertos, or Day of the Dead. It's a festival that celebrates family and friends who have died. People decorate special altars and cemeteries with photographs, along with orange marigolds, and colorful sugar skulls.

It is a joyful holiday that helps the living remember the people they love. They tell funny stories and share happy memories.

Take time to share a happy memory of someone you love today.

NOVEMBER 3
EAT A SANDWICH

Sandwiches are full of joy. Whether you have the same kind for lunch every day or you only eat them once in a while, a sandwich really hits the spot when you're hungry.

What kind of sandwiches do you like?

Toastie

Ham and cheese

Peanut butter
and jelly

Ask around today, "What's your favorite sandwich?"

NOVEMBER 4
ADMIRE GINKGO TREES

Ginkgo trees are beautiful. They have fan-shaped leaves that look delicate. In fact, gingko trees are very strong and can live for more than a thousand years.

In autumn, the leaves on a ginkgo tree turn a beautiful yellow that glows in the sunlight. They tend to fall all at the same time, covering the earth in gold. Isn't that magnificent?

NOVEMBER 5
CHOOSE A DOUGHNUT

Doughnuts are both simple and a bit fancy.

A box of doughnuts is joyful, like scattered confetti, a bunch of balloons, or polka-dotted wrapping paper!

What kind of doughnut would you choose to eat today?

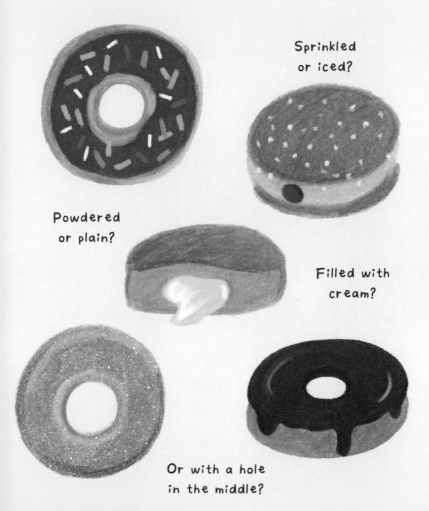

Sprinkled or iced?

Powdered or plain?

Filled with cream?

Or with a hole in the middle?

NOVEMBER 6
BEFRIEND A FISH

Fish have all kinds of noses, fins, and tails.
Notice their stunning colors and patterns.

Fish are calming to watch, easy to care
for, and are really good listeners.

Try talking to some fish today.
You could tell them a joke!
Do they laugh and swim away?

NOVEMBER 7
VOTE!

Voting is an important right. It gives us power to choose what we want and who we want. Voting is a way for many people to make a big decision in a fair way.

Our votes make a difference!

NOVEMBER 8
TEACH WHAT YOU KNOW

Did you know that you know a lot?
Teach a friend something you know.
It could be a new skill, subject, trick, or game.

Sharing what you know is a special way
to connect with a friend.

NOVEMBER 9
DO A CARTWHEEL

Spread your arms and legs out like a star and kick into a cartwheel.

Can't quite do one yet? Keep practicing!

When you get it, you'll be so happy, you'll want to . . . do a cartwheel!

NOVEMBER 10
PLAY HIDE-AND-SEEK

What's your favorite part of playing hide-and-seek?
Do you like finding a super-hidden spot that no one
can find? Do you like popping out of hiding at the
end of the game? Or do you like catching all
of your friends?

Play a game of hide-and-seek today and
enjoy all the parts!

NOVEMBER 11
MAKE A HILARIOUS VIDEO

What could you do to make someone chuckle today?
Try using a camera phone to make a funny video.
Make silly faces, sing a song, tell a joke,
or do something surprising.

Does your video make you giggle? Great!
Send it to someone to brighten their day.

NOVEMBER 12
PAINT PINE CONES

Go for a walk and collect pine cones.

Gather some craft supplies.

Experiment by rolling pine cones in paint,
glueing on googly eyes, or stringing them together.

Make something that will delight you today.
You can also give away what you make to
delight a friend.

NOVEMBER 13
WORLD KINDNESS DAY

Light up the world with kindness today.

At home, offer your help.
Around town, give a compliment.
At the playground, invite someone to go ahead of you.
You can be kind anywhere.

NOVEMBER 14
EAT SOMETHING SOUR

Eating sour things can excite your taste buds.

Today, try tasting a sour food such as a lemon, cranberries, tamarind, kimchi, or sauerkraut.

See if it makes you pucker your lips, squeal, and howl with glee.

NOVEMBER 15
PAINT LIKE GEORGIA O'KEEFFE

Georgia O'Keeffe was born on this date in 1887.
She was an American artist who was inspired by nature.
She loved the deserts of New Mexico and painted
bold, beautiful pictures.

What things in nature are beautiful to you?

What inspires you?
What makes you want to draw or paint?

DECORATE WITH POLKA DOTS

A polka-dot pattern feels like a party.

Try decorating with polka dots today.

You can make wrapping paper or a greetings card.
You could decorate a lunch bag or a letter.
You could even use fabric markers and
design a pillowcase or T-shirt.

What combination of polka-dot colors makes
you feel happy?

NOVEMBER 17
EXPLORE ROCKS AND MINERALS

Rocks and minerals come in a variety of shapes,
textures, and colors. Which ones appeal to your eyes?
Which ones do you like to hold in your hand?

Some people think that holding rocks or crystals can
help you feel calm, creative, energetic, and happy.

NOVEMBER 18
SING IN THE SHOWER

Have you ever sung in the shower or while taking a bath?

Sing a song that makes you feel good
and sing it loud today!

There's something about singing in the bathroom
that makes your voice sound even better.

NOVEMBER 19
BREATHE LIKE A LION

Sometimes big feelings can feel too big. Try breathing like a lion when big feelings like frustration or excitement take over.

Take a slow breath through your nose.
Fill your belly with air.
Then open your mouth wide . . .
Stretch out your tongue . . .
And breathe out as strong as a lion's mighty roar.

Breathing can calm our body, so we feel ready to do things that make us happy!

NOVEMBER 20
WORLD CHILDREN'S DAY

World Children's Day is held every year on this day around the world. Today is all about the importance of children, just like you, and how they have special rights and freedoms that help them to grow into happy, healthy adults.

Learn about children's rights today and share your knowledge with others to help spread awareness.

NOVEMBER 21
CLIMB HIGH

Reach your hand.
Place your foot.

Push down.
Pull up.

Hold on tight.
Check your balance.

Keep going!
Enjoy the view.

NOVEMBER 22
SHARE YOUR WORRIES

Everyone feels worried or has bad dreams sometimes.

In Guatemala, children can tell their worries to special handmade dolls. A legend says the dolls can take the worries away.

Talking to others can help us feel less sad and scared. Who can you talk to when you feel worried?

NOVEMBER 23
GO UPSIDE DOWN

Need a pick-me-up? Go upside down!

Look through your legs.
Stand on your head.
Do a handstand.
Flip your view.

Going upside down can make you feel
light-headed and light-hearted.

BAKE WITH AUTUMN FOODS

Autumn is full of delightful flavors.

Try baking something that features
an autumn food today.

Apples into
apple crumble

Pumpkins into
pumpkin bread

Pecans into
pecan sticky buns

Pears into
a pear tart

Notice how the kitchen smells when goodies are in the
oven. Then, enjoy every bite of what you baked!

NOVEMBER 25
GIVE THANKS

Thanksgiving is an American holiday
celebrated in November.

It's a time to be together,
eat together,
play together,
laugh together.

What are you especially thankful for this year?

NOVEMBER 26
READ COMICS

On this day in 1922, Charles Schulz was born in Minnesota. When Charles was young, all he wanted to do was draw funny pictures. So, he did!

Charles created Peanuts, a comic strip featuring a boy named Charlie Brown and a dog named Snoopy. He told stories that were funny, happy, and even disappointing, just like life can be sometimes.

Read some comics today, or write your own!

NOVEMBER 27
LEARN A NEW LANGUAGE

Learning different languages helps us discover
fascinating people and places.

Here's how you can say "thank you" in . . .

Arabic:
shukran
(shoe-kran)

Korean:
kamsahamnida
(kam-sah-ham-nee-da)

Japanese:
arigato
(ah-ree-gah-toe)

Russian:
spasiba
(spuh-see-buh)

Norwegian:
takk
(tahk)

Hawaiian:
mahalo
(ma-ha-lo)

Spanish:
gracias
(grah-syahs)

What words do you know in other languages?
Who could you talk to in another language?

NOVEMBER 28
LIGHT A CANDLE

Hanukkah is a Jewish holiday celebrated for eight nights. Normally it occurs between late November and December, although the exact dates change every year. Families gather together to light candles on the menorah. They sing songs and say prayers.

Candles can symbolize faith, miracles, and wishes.
Do candles remind you of anything joyful?
For what happy occasions do you light candles?

NOVEMBER 29
VISIT A LOCAL SHOP

Is there a store that you enjoy browsing in?

Maybe it smells delicious, has aisles of art supplies you can't wait to try out, has shelves of books you can't wait to read, or has displays for things that you don't even know what they're for!

Walk around and see what makes you curious.
What makes you want to pick something up
and look at it closer?

NOVEMBER 30
PLANT A GRATITUDE TREE

Look back at the things you've been grateful for this past month. Why don't you check your gratitude jar?

Use your collection to make a gratitude tree and watch your joy bloom.

DECEMBER 1
COUNTDOWN CALENDAR

For Christian people, today is the beginning of the
Advent season. Advent is the time leading up
to Christmas.

The first Advent calendars were produced in the 1800s
in Germany. It's now common for children all around the
world to have Advent calendars to count down the days.
The dates are featured on small windows and on each
day, you pop open the window to find a little treat.

What are you looking forward to this December?
Write it on a calendar today and enjoy counting down.

DECEMBER 2
ENJOY THE SMELLS
OF THE SEASON

What scents make you feel at home?
Take a deep breath and savor each smell.

Pine trees

Roasted chestnuts

Gingerbread

Chocolate

Clementines

DECEMBER 3
INTERNATIONAL DAY OF PERSONS WITH DISABILITIES

Some of us wear glasses or hearing aids.
Some of us use wheelchairs to get around,
all or some of the time.
Some of us read with our eyes.
Some of us read with our fingers.
Some of us communicate with our mouths.
Some of us communicate with our bodies.

Today is the International
Day of Persons with
Disabilities.

What are some
things that all
people have in
common?

DECEMBER 4
SPOT DECEMBER BLOOMS

Plants that bloom in spring get a lot of attention.
Did you know that lots of beautiful plants bloom in
autumn and winter, too?

Plants that flourish in autumn and winter are strong and
resilient. Throughout the colder seasons, look for dots
of color, indoors and out!

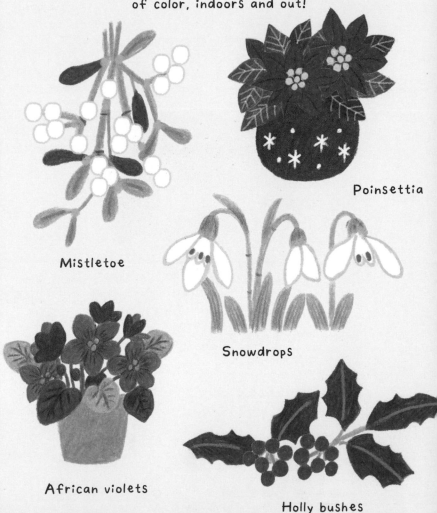

Mistletoe

Poinsettia

Snowdrops

African violets

Holly bushes

DECEMBER 5
PRACTICE MARTIAL ARTS

Kick! Punch! Block!

Different countries have developed their own styles of martial arts over thousands of years. Practicing martial arts builds strength, balance, flexibility, concentration, memory, and confidence!

Do you know any martial arts moves?
Practice or learn a new one today.

What kinds of activities make you feel
focused and confident?

DECEMBER 6
DECORATE A CHRISTMAS TREE

String the lights,
Twinkly lights.
Drape the tinsel,
Sparkly tinsel.

Hang the ornaments,
Favorite ornaments.
Place the star,
Shining star.

Christmas trees bring Christmas cheer!

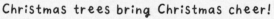

DECEMBER 7
FEEL THE MAGIC OF A SHOW

There are all kinds of enchanting shows during December,
such as choral concerts, carols and big brass bands!

Whether you're standing on the stage or watching
with the crowd, feel under a magic spell.

What feels magical to you in December?

DECEMBER 8
MAKE PAPER SNOWFLAKES

The snowy season is coming. Or maybe it's already here!
It doesn't matter where you live, you can always
make snow.

Gather some paper and a pair of scissors to make your
own snowy day today.

Don't worry if your paper snowflake isn't perfect.
No two snowflakes are ever alike.

DECEMBER 9
GO ON A NEIGHBORHOOD STROLL

What decorations do you see around
your neighborhood this time of year?

Are there places that look especially merry?
Go on a scavenger hunt to find decorations you see year
after year as well as decorations you've never seen before.
Point out what you find to family and friends.

DECEMBER 10
LOVE TO LEARN LIKE ADA LOVELACE

On this date in 1815, Ada Lovelace was born in London, England. Ada grew up using her imagination to design boats and machines. As a grown-up, Ada realized that machines could do things no one had ever imagined before. They could calculate numbers. They could do things like make music and pictures, too. Ada combined all the things she loved learning about with her imagination. She is known as the mother of modern computing and the first computer programmer.

What are three things that you like to learn about? Your unique interests could change the world someday. Wouldn't that be incredible?

DECEMBER 11
INTERNATIONAL MOUNTAIN DAY

Mountains are majestic. Today is an international day
to embrace the wonder of the mountains around us.

Make a plan to reach the top of a mountain
or anywhere with an awesome view.

Plant your feet on the ground,
your hands on your hips,
and stretch up tall.
Imagine you are as strong as a mountain.

Sometimes we can feel big or small depending on what's
around us. No matter where we are, our size is just right.

DECEMBER 12
SPREAD CHEER

In 1931, most people in New York City didn't have much money. With the holidays coming up, the Rockefeller Center workers put their money together to buy a Christmas tree which cheered up the people around them.

Now Rockefeller Center has a Christmas tree every year. While the first tree was 20 feet tall, the trees since have been as tall as 100 feet. When the tree is taken down, it's turned into wood that is used to build homes for people who need them. Isn't that wonderful?

The tree symbolizes the Christmas spirit for millions. You never know what one thoughtful action can do.

DECEMBER 13
ROOT FOR A TEAM

What sports do you like watching?
Do you have a team that you follow?
Watch a game and cheer for your team today!

It's fun to be a fan and gather with people
who love the same thing as you.

DECEMBER 14
EAT SOUP

Mmm . . . hot soup on a cold winter day is the best.
Tomato soup
French onion soup
Lentil soup
Miso soup

What kind
of soup do
you like?

DECEMBER 15
WATCH A SUNSET

Notice the changes in nature as the season
moves from autumn to winter.

Gaze around at sunset.
What do the trees look like?
Are there leaves or empty branches?
What's on the ground?

Look up into the sky.
Do you see any birds flying south?
What do the clouds look like?
What colors would you use to paint the sky?

Name something that makes you happy when the weather
is colder.

DECEMBER 16
LISTEN TO FAMILY STORIES

Many people are spending time with aunts, uncles,
grandparents, and cousins this time of year.
Ask relatives to tell family stories.

What things made them happy when they were your age?
What did they do for fun when they were young?

352

DECEMBER 17
MAKE A GIFT

December is the season of giving. Make a handmade gift for someone you care about today.

You could make:

A piece of art for an empty wall.

A painted planter for a garden of herbs.

CLAY

A pinch pot to place coins and keys.

Your thoughtfulness is a great way to give joy.

DECEMBER 18
BAKE COOKIES

Baking cookies is fun anytime.
It's especially fun during the holidays.

Bake some cookies today.
Keep some and give some!
Pick out a yummy selection.
Put them in a bag or tin.
Write a note.
Deliver your goodies.

TO OUR POSTAL WORKERS

TO OUR FIRE FIGHTERS

Eating cookies is great. Sharing cookies is joyful.

DECEMBER 19
AUTUMN FAVORITES

The winter solstice is coming up.

Take a look outside and see how things have changed.
Flip through your tree pictures from September.
Touch your collection of leaves from October.
Remember what you were grateful for in November.
Look in the mirror. See how you've changed this autumn.

DECEMBER 20
HAVE A MOVIE MARATHON

When it's getting colder outside, it's fun to get
cozy inside. Pick a film, dim the lights, curl up
on the sofa with your family.

What film makes you laugh together?
Do you have a special film that you like
to watch at this time of year?

Dalphin MOVIE

CHRISTMAS MOVIE

DECEMBER 21
WELCOME WINTER

For places in the northern hemisphere, today marks the winter solstice and first day of winter. It's the shortest day of the year with the longest night.

During the late afternoon, go stand outside. Notice how long your shadow is. You look so tall! Grab some chalk and a tape measure and invite someone to join you. Take turns tracing each other's shadows and measuring them. On the winter solstice, the sun's low position in the sky makes our shadows extra long.

We can see the wonders of the universe in our very own shadows.

DECEMBER 22
SEARCH FOR SHADES OF BLUE

There are so many rich shades of blue in the world.
See how many you can spot today.

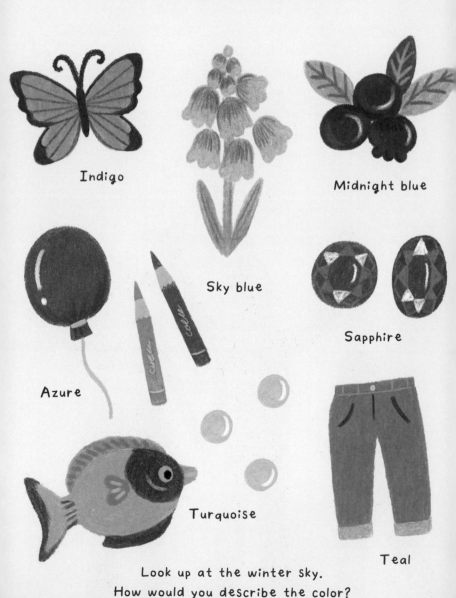

Indigo

Midnight blue

Sky blue

Sapphire

Azure

Turquoise

Teal

Look up at the winter sky.
How would you describe the color?

DECEMBER 23
VISIT A WINTER MARKET

Have you ever been to a winter market?
Look for one near you.

Roam the stalls to see beautiful crafts, scrumptious
foods, and other handmade goodies.

Discover lots of unique and creative things people enjoy
making. Look for ideas for things you'd enjoy making, too!

HOMEMADE
Cookies
& CAKES♥

HOT
COCOA

DECEMBER 24
SEE YOUR BREATH

What's the weather like today?

Take a deep breath in and breathe it out slowly.
Do you see frosty breath?

Smell the air.
Do you smell snow?

Touch your rosy cheeks.
How does the winter air feel on your skin?

DECEMBER 25
CHRISTMAS

For those who celebrate it, Christmas is a day
filled with joy from morning until night.

Cherish all the thoughtful gifts, yummy food, and time
with the people you love and who love you.

Merry Christmas!

DECEMBER 26
KWANZAA

Kwanzaa is a holiday celebrated by some African
Americans from today until January 1. It celebrates
seven principles, including creativity, unity, and faith.
The festivities last for seven days and there
are seven symbols.

Kinara: candleholder
Mazao: crops
Mkeka: mat
Muhindi: corn
Kikombe cha Umoja: unity cup
Zawadi: gifts
Mishumaa Saba: seven candles

When we have unity and community, all people can be more
joyful. What symbolizes unity or community to you?

DECEMBER 27
PLAY VIDEO GAMES

Too cold outside today?
Play some video games!

Work together.
Challenge another.
Play by yourself.

Have a good time!

DECEMBER 28
RAINBOW HUNT

Finding a rainbow can fill us with joy.
Take part in a rainbow hunt today.

Look for items around your home that are
red, orange, yellow, green, blue, and purple.
Draw or write about what you find.

You can always find a rainbow when you look hard enough.

DECEMBER 29
GO SLEDDING

Take a ride down a snowy hill.

Pull your sled up the hill.
Trudge, trudge, tug, tug.
Ready . . . steady . . .
Push off and go!
Wheeeee!

The climb is hard work. The ride is worth it!

DECEMBER 30
APPRECIATE YOUR COLLECTIONS

Do you have a collection of treasures? Maybe you have a special container to keep them in. Or maybe you can find things that are special to you all around your bedroom.

Take a few minutes to go through and hold each one. Why are they special to you? Do they remind you of:

An exciting moment?

A loving moment?

A creative moment?

A moment in nature?

Keep collecting little bits of joy in your heart and mind each and every day. It helps you find, grow, and feel joy that lasts the whole year and more!

DECEMBER 31
NEW YEAR'S EVE

Many countries have special customs on New Year's Eve.

In Spain and the Philippines, people eat twelve grapes at midnight. The round-shaped fruit symbolizes coins and good fortune.

In the Netherlands, it's a tradition to watch fireworks and eat oliebollen, warm crispy balls of fried dough dusted in sugar.

In Greece, people hang onions on their front doors. The onions symbolize rebirth for the new year.

New Year's Eve is so unique. It's the ending of one year and the beginning of the next one. It's an ideal time to soak in the wonderful memories from the past and carry them into the future.

Happy New Year!

The illustrations in this book were created digitally.
Set in Annelies Pen, Quicksand, and Sofa Sans.

Library of Congress Control Number 2020952011
ISBN 978-1-4197-5285-8

First published in the United Kingdom in 2021 by Magic Cat Publishing Ltd.
First published in North America in 2021 by Magic Cat Publishing, an imprint
of ABRAMS. All rights reserved. No portion of this book may be reproduced,
stored in a retrieval system, or transmitted in any form or by any means,
mechanical, electronic, photocopying, recording, or otherwise, without
written permission from the publisher.

Printed and bound in China
10 9 8 7 6 5 4 3 2

Abrams Books are available at special discounts when purchased in quantity
for premiums and promotions
as well as fundraising or educational use. Special editions can also be
created to specification. For details, contact specialsales@abramsbooks.
com or the address below.

ABRAMS The Art of Books
195 Broadway, New York, NY 10007
abramsbooks.com